UNHAPPY
SECRETS
OF THE
CHRISTIAN
LIFE

UNHAPPY SECRETS OF THE CHRISTIAN LIFE

Philip Yancey & Tim Stafford

ZONDERVAN PUBLISHING HOUSE
OF THE ZONDERVAN CORPORATION
GRAND RAPIDS, MICHIGAN 49506

CAMPUS LIFE BOOKS
A DIVISION OF YOUTH FOR CHRIST
WHEATON, ILLINOIS 60187

We acknowledge the publishers of the following passages quoted in this book:

Of Human Bondage, by W. Somerset Maugham, © 1915 Doubleday & Co., © 1950 by Pocket Books, Inc., New York, pages 26-30.

Adventures of Huckleberry Finn, by Samuel Clemens, Smalfield Publishing Co., Akron, Ohio, 1941, page 21.

Library of Congress Cataloging in Publication Data

Yancey, Philip.
  Unhappy secrets of the Christian life..

  "A Campus life book."
  1. Christian life—Addresses, essays, lectures.
I. Stafford, Tim, joint author.   II. Title.
BV4501.2.Y32   248'.4   78-26460
ISBN 0-310-35420-X: cloth
ISBN 0-310-35421-8: paper

Printed in the United States of America

Contents

Foreword

A dangerous rumor is making the rounds. It's the notion that problems fade away when you become a Christian. We've found that idea to be totally false. Although the new life in Christ brings with it much joy and happiness, it also involves a new set of struggles.

As J. B. Phillips reminded us, "It is only when we are going in more or less the same direction as the devil that we are unconscious of any opposition at all." During our time as editors of CAMPUS LIFE we have heard from thousands of readers about specific problems they've encountered. Their experience, as well as our own, assures us that this book is necessary.

We can practically guarantee that you'll run into each of these "unhappy secrets," if you haven't already. We sincerely hope these shared thoughts will act as a "vaccination" to prepare you for you own battles.

—Philip Yancey and Tim Stafford

UNHAPPY SECRETS
OF THE
CHRISTIAN LIFE

Seeing the
Invisible

by Philip Yancey

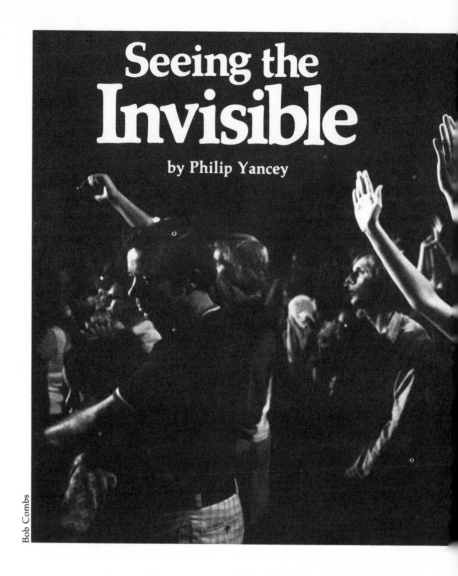

**Naturalism: How do you keep believing
in something you can't see,
touch, smell, or prove?**

■ I've met some weird Christians . . . really weird, especially when I was in college. One guy named Samuel (he would never let you call him Sam) was a fantastic tennis player. Because he thought tennis was a little unspiritual, you would have to coax him into playing. On the court he was a demon (he would never let you call him that, either!): smashing backhands, looping high, precise lobs, demolishing the ball with an overhead slam.

Instead of cursing, Samuel reserved a nice Christian-sounding word to shout just before creaming the ball. About every fourth serve, his back would arch more steeply than usual, he would toss the ball higher and his feet would leave the ground. Just before his arm whipped forward to whack the ball, he'd grunt loudly, "'Lujah!!"

I still shudder when I think of that word "'lujah." Maybe Samuel meant it as an expression of his faith in God. But to me it was a final warning to dodge a missile which would come screaming over the net and kick up into my face.

Though Samuel was pretty weird, he earned respect in almost any crowd by his inspired tennis playing. Brian was the opposite—the butt of everyone's jokes. His 130 pounds were stretched along a 6'4" frame and, maybe because he didn't have enough strength to hold himself up, he walked with a permanent forward bend, as if he had carried a heavy backpack during all his growing years.

Brian talked shyly and softly, and his face was so pale and fragile that you couldn't help mentally picturing him as a ghost. To compound matters, Brian had the peculiar habit of walking around on his toes, backward, memorizing Bible verses. That's the truth. Every night he would dress in a white sweatsuit, jog a loping mile, then cool off by walking in circles under a streetlight, *backward*. It was an eerie scene: Brian's forward-tilting body jerking backward along the perimeter of the streetlight's glow, his head bowed, straining to see the verse he'd printed on a card, mumbling to himself.

I admit, not all the Christians I knew were as weird as Samuel and Brian. But those two were given a special level of respect among Christians as if their "'lujah"-shouting and backward-walking-verse-memorizing elevated them to a special class. At the Christian college I attended, most people thought them more "spiritual" than others. Knowing them, I kept asking myself, "Is this what God wants?"

All the Christians, however, from Debbie, the blonde knockout, to George, the math expert, shared some traits which seemed at first to me every bit as weird as Samuel and Brian's eccentricities.

There was prayer, for example. Christians I knew distorted events to make everything look like an answer to prayer. If an uncle sent an extra $25 for school bills, they would grin and shout and call a prayer meeting to thank God for it. While sane people on campus were sleeping off the night's activities, the super-Christians would sneak out of their rooms at 6:30 A.M. for a prayer meeting.

They seemed to take these "answers to prayer" as final proof that a God was out there listening to them. I could always find some other explanation for them. "Maybe that uncle sent *all* his nephews $25 this month," I would say. "Some of the nephews aren't Christians. Was yours the only gift that answered a prayer?" They never discussed the frequent times God ignored their specific requests. Prayer, to me, was a foolish activity. Of what use was talking aloud to the walls?

But the super-Christians' earnestness dumbfounded me. Partly out of curiosity and partly out of a malicious desire to destroy their illusions, I started hanging around them, even acting "Christian." I made up some story about how I had gotten "saved" as a teenager, embellished it with dramatic details, and told it at one of the Christian sharing meetings. The response was unbelievable. Most of the girls were in tears. Everyone hugged me, said "Praise God!" and had a special prayer meeting of gratitude.

I began attending the prayer meetings—even the early morning eyeproppers—and whatever the best Christians did, I would imitate. I learned the key to acceptance was a ritual called "giving your testimony" in which your voice took on a soft, sincere tone and you told of some way the Lord had blessed you or "spoken to you." I found after a few weeks that I was one of the best testimony-givers of the bunch. I could often bring the group to prayers of thanksgiving, or beckon tears from their hungry, searching eyes.

Meanwhile, I would race back to the dorm after these sessions and tell my real friends how thoroughly I was hoodwinking all the Christians. In my mind, I had devastated their faith. I was a naturalist, and I believed there was no God. The only world existing was the world I lived in: rocks, trees, and air. There were no "spiritual beings." Obviously their

John Chao

I found myself mumbling the same, imprecise phrases, like, "God completely transformed me," or "God has changed my whole way of thinking."

faith comprised spiritual jargon, a warm feeling of closeness, and a guilt trip all thrown together. Though an avowed unbeliever, I could pass for a veritable saint just by following the prescribed formula. Theirs was no different from any other misguided religion. How could God be real if all Christian experience could be duplicated by someone who did not believe in him?

A strange thing happened about a year after this experiment. It would have been humiliating and embarrassing had it not been so overwhelmingly delightful. I became a Christian. God met me in an amazing, undeniable way, at a time when I wasn't even looking for him—in fact, while I was hotly denying him. I experienced a true Christian conversion. During a routine (required) prayer meeting with friends, God made contact with me. He showed me his love and forgiveness, and I was born again.

Though I had spent my energy to that point trying to poke holes in the Christian faith and sniff out inconsistencies in Christians, when God finally met me the change was so profound that I have never doubted it since.

How could I describe this experience to my skeptical friends whom I had succeeded in pushing toward agnosticism? How do you describe a world of color to someone born color-blind? I found myself mumbling the same imprecise phrases, like "God completely transformed me" or "God has changed my whole way of thinking, my sense of values" or "He's given me peace I have never known before." Most of my friends looked at me with an unknowing, confused, even *betrayed* look. I knew what they were thinking: "It's finally gotten to the poor fellow. After months of hanging around those super-Christians, imitating them, he cracked. He's loony."

Frustrated, I tried to think of ways to persuade my friends that I had not gone loony but rather had found a deeper reality. I knew they wouldn't be attracted to the Christians I knew—I had mocked them too successfully. The idea of miracles came to me. Could I find some absolutely unexplainable miracle? Surely that would prove God's reality.

Why wasn't God more obvious? I wanted him to conduct well-orchestrated, televised miracles so that I could invite my skeptical friends to see an act of God they could never deny.

The problem, as I saw it, was that the Christian acts—praying, loving each other, sharing faith with others, worshiping—just weren't *supernatural* enough to convince anyone that Christianity is true. *What we really need*, I thought, *is a giant, world-wide awesome display of God's power.* Naturalism would topple to the ground.

Even as I thought that, I realized it wouldn't work. The Bible records scores of instances when God really shocked the world. The ten plagues of Egypt, for example. Cecil B. DeMille spent millions to imitate them, and his film sequences still look phony. What of the resurrection of Jesus? More than five hundred people attested that he had come back from the dead, but most people refused to believe them. God himself walked on earth for thirty three years, teaching and performing astounding miracles. Yet, of those who heard him, only a minority believed.

Miracles—the wide-open, fireworks, supernatural sort—will always be an exception. Oh, I believe they occur. Many of my friends tell me of some miraculous healing, or a dramatic change God worked in a drug addict. But those miracles which suspend the laws of nature for an instant—I must admit I have never seen one personally.

I don't need miracles to believe; God has lovingly proved himself to me. It only bothers me when I think about my skeptical friends. If God really did a miracle, right in front of their eyes, would they believe? I don't know.

Instead I am left with the simple, sometimes tedious Christian acts of praying, sharing, loving, serving. As I know too well from my early contacts with weird Christians, those acts fall short of convincing a skeptic. They can even be expertly duplicated as a joke or as a sociology experiment.

I never did come up with a good strategy for convincing skeptics. Some came to believe, some didn't. Some were attracted to God by Christians' love; some fled to him when their world was crumbling. Many others, though, are far from God today.

Today, even after all God has done for me, I have doubts. I will always believe he's real. But often my prayers seem like hollow, sleepy words that bounce off walls and rise no higher than my ceiling. Sometimes when I hear a fellow Christian describe an experience he has had with the Lord, it sounds no different from what you might hear at a Transcendental Meditation meeting or in an encounter group. It is still sometimes hard for me to believe—*really* believe—that there is another part of the world out there. I am never completely rid of naturalism, because the only world I *see* everyday is the natural one. How do I keep believing in an invisible world?

There is an evident world around me, comprising trees and rocks and people and cars and buildings. Everyone believes in that one. But there is an equally real world of angels and spirits and God and heaven and hell. If only I could see that other world, just once, perhaps that would solve all my doubts.

When those doubts surface, I think back to some of Jesus' teaching about the two worlds. One incident (in Luke 10) especially pulled the two worlds together. Jesus sent out seventy of his faithful followers to the towns and villages he planned to visit later. He warned them sternly that they might be mocked or even persecuted for representing him. "You are like lambs among wolves," he said.

The seventy disciples trudged away in the dust, certainly expecting the worst after Jesus' pessimistic warnings. But they returned exuberant. People had accepted them. Towns were eagerly awaiting the visit of Jesus. They had healed sick people. "Even the demons submit to us in your name," they breathlessly reported.

Jesus, who had been waiting for their return, gave a unique summary of what had happened. He said, "I saw Satan fall like lightning from heaven!" Jesus brought the two worlds together. The world of the disciples had been one of walking over hot sand, preaching to mixed crowds, knocking on doors, asking to see the sick, announcing the coming of Jesus. All their actions took place in the visible world which you can touch, smell, and see. But Jesus, with supernatural insight, saw that those actions in the visible world were having a phenomenal impact on the invisible world. While disciples were grinding out spiritual victories in the visible world, Satan was falling to their onslaught in the invisible world.

In Luke 12, Jesus gave some more clues that what happens

here in the visible world affects the other world. He said that whatever we whisper in the inner rooms, thinking we are alone and safe, will one day be broadcast from the housetops for all to hear. No act, even whispering, is going unnoticed in

Jim Whitmer

Cafeteria Talk
by L. Fischer

■ You know the sound of a cafeteria. The rattling of plates and silverware. The dull roar of a dozen conversations. But somehow you don't notice the sound when you're helping to make it.

Today Sol and I are talking in the cafeteria of an African university. Sol is black and African and very proud of it. I am a white American, trying to learn about Africa. We met in a class we have together.

He often brings up the subject of religion. He knows I'm a Christian. "But it's a cultural thing," he says. "Christianity is a part of your culture, not mine. Christianity is not for Africa, and it's not for me."

So here we are again, talking about religion over a Coke.

Sol objects to what he has seen in Christianity in the past. Christian missionaries and white colonialists in general exploited his people, looking down on them with a superior attitude. Sol explains, "The missionaries told us, 'Your way of life is inferior to ours. The way you dress is inferior. Your color is inferior. Your language is inferior.' They even

UNHAPPY SECRETS OF THE CHRISTIAN LIFE

the world. Each is recording its mark in the invisible world.

Jesus said that when a sinner repents, the angels in heaven rejoice. Today you can watch a sinner repent. Turn on a Billy Graham crusade sometime and you can see, live in color,

advised us to discard our African names. They said, 'Change your names to the names of Bible characters or great Christians from Europe or America. Turn to God, and you will be like us.'

"But they are hypocrites," Sol continues—"missionaries and African Christians alike. What they say and what they do are two different things. They say we should live morally. But *they* don't. They say Christians should love each other. But they don't love, and they don't care. And when I needed help, they wouldn't help me. I came to the city to go to school. I had no income, no place to stay, no friends. I went to the Christians and they turned me away."

Sol's experiences were real. I had heard stories like his before. But I wish he knew some of the other Christians I have met in Africa.

I wish Sol knew people like Audu, the young professional man who read the New Testament, was impressed by its emphasis on love, and decided to become a Christian. Audu knew he might be killed for rejecting the religion of his family. He was afraid to go back home. But he did return to his people because he wanted to share God's love with them.

By now Sol and I have finished our Cokes, but we continue to talk. He asks me questions, and I ask him questions. And in the discussion I mention that a Christian has Christ in him and . . .

Sol interrupts. His voice is deliberate and challenging. "Do you really think Christ is in you?"

"Well . . . " (I wasn't expecting that.) "Well . . . yes."

And Sol leans back in his chair and laughs. Not just a little snicker, but a long, deep laugh, really letting it go.

Then I start laughing too. I guess it really does sound funny. I mean, here I am saying that *God,* the one who made the whole world and keeps it going, is in *me.* Me, sitting here on a chair in the cafeteria. Me, with my notebook lying on the table next to me.

I wonder if Sol can see Christ in me. ∎

many sinners repenting. The camera zooms in on a middle-aged businessman, head lowered, threading his way down the stadium seats to talk to a counselor. It moves to a young girl, in Levis and an army jacket, quietly sobbing in a corner as a friend explains the Bible to her. According to what Jesus said, while those visible acts are taking place, some tremendous invisible acts are also occurring. The angels are throwing a celebration in heaven. The two worlds are working as one.

Jesus continued, "I tell you, whoever acknowledges me before men, the Son of Man will also acknowledge him before the angels of God. But he who disowns me before men will be disowned before the angels of God."

The man Jesus was, of course, the ultimate example of the two worlds working as one. He was a man with sweat glands, hair, fingernails, lips, and all the characteristics which define humans. Yet inside that body, God lived.

All of us who are Christians believe in the invisible world; we merely forget it. We get consumed by our world of arguments, relationships, jobs, and school—and even the "religious" world of church and prayer meetings. Perhaps if Jesus were standing in the flesh beside us, murmuring phrases like "I saw Satan fall" whenever God used us for some good, we would remember better.

The world we live in is not an either/or world. The actions I do as a Christian—praying, worshiping, loving—are not exclusively supernatural or natural. They are both, working at the same time.

As reminders of the supernatural world we are given God's Spirit, who permanently dwells within us. We are given the

Ed Wallowitch

Do you wish to see expression of God's power?
Get up early to watch a sunrise or visit California beaches
during whale migrating season.

UNHAPPY SECRETS OF THE CHRISTIAN LIFE

good counsel of the Bible and of fellow Christians, who affirm with us that, yes, there is another world, and God is alive and cares about us.

Besides all these specifically Christian reminders, there are many rumors of God in the world which can be detected by everyone. Do you wish to see expression of God's power? Get up early to watch a sunrise. Visit California beaches during whale migrating season and watch the great beasts frolic and sputter.

Do you question whether man is immortal? Consider your own reaction when you pass a dead cat or skunk or oppossum on the road. You may feel a twinge of regret or sadness, especially if you love animals; it is not at all the reaction you would feel if you passed a human body sprawled next to the pavement. You would gasp and screech to a halt. The memory would burn into your mind. You would never forget the scene. What is the difference? Both corpses are made of sinew, blood, bone, and organs. The difference is nothing visible; it is the fact that the person is immortal, made in God's image.

Sometimes I remember the invisible world clearly. I can sense its existence so strongly that it seems more real than the visible world. The quality of *faith* lets me believe—the quality that the Book of Hebrews defines as "the substance of things hoped for, the evidence of things not seen." At those moments (I remember how I felt after my conversion) I wonder how anyone could doubt. Other times—often when I'm tired and irritable, and have just fought with someone—I can barely remember the invisible world. Those moments, too, are symptoms of the great spiritual struggle going on behind the curtain, accompanying every moment of my life.

"There is no neutral ground in the universe," said C. S. Lewis. "Every inch, every split second, is claimed by God and counter-claimed by Satan."

I am strong enough to believe that on my own sometimes. I feel very much a part of a battle. But at other times I forget and must be pressed back to God, to his Word, to the helpless dependence on him and his followers here on earth. They remind me of the invisible world and my role in it. Satan does not give up his ground easily. ∎

Temptation:
When what looks good is bad.

The Squeeze

by Tim Stafford

■ Do you know what unhappy secret I find more discouraging than anything else in my life? It's the feeling I get right after I have given in, again, to temptation—after I go into a self-pitying sulk or look at a dirty magazine.

I have no doubt about forgiveness. I know that God will take away the sin and make me new. But I wonder if I will ever escape temptation. When it comes down to it, do I really have any strength to resist? I can picture myself failing again and again and again.

So I have thought about temptation, wondering if there is a key, a magic secret, to resisting it. "Yielding to God" or "turning to the Lord" are phrases that have helped at times. But I have found there is no magic in phrases. I cannot turn away from temptation just by putting myself through some mental gymnastics.

Religious "techniques" have left me very discouraged. I will think I have the answer. Then, giving in to temptation again, I will abruptly know that I don't.

It has helped, though, to think through the nature of temptation. Is there some consistent trend I can discern in it? I have found three different components to temptation, and all three must be dealt with at once.

Temptation can be a physical object you encounter.
Temptation is a beautiful woman you can easily turn into an object instead of a person, by letting her body preoccupy your thoughts.
Temptation is a piece of pie when you are trying to lose weight.
Temptation is a pornographic magazine.

Richard Nowitz

Temptation is too much change returned by a cashier.

If you want to avoid temptation, avoid these objects as much as you possibly can. Unfortunately, some of those objects are not easy to stay away from without becoming a hermit.

Temptation is a pressure situation, when everyone kids you and eggs you to do something you would rather not.

Temptation is when your boss jumps on your back, and you feel like lashing out at him or her.

Temptation is when you are in a group of strangers who are laughing and having a good time among themselves, and you feel like creeping away and feeling sorry for yourself.

In other words, temptation comes with pressure situations. By yourself you might not want to do the things toward which those situations tempt you. You wouldn't gossip if you weren't around friends who were gossiping. You wouldn't swear if your friends didn't.

Some of those situations you can stay away from, just as you can stay away from tempting objects. If a group of friends is constantly in trouble, you may need to find new friends or you can keep away from them at the times when they're out for trouble.

Other situations you may be able to defuse. One well-placed remark may loosen up a tense moment. You can become a leader in your group instead of a follower. You can sit down with your boss and explain how you feel so that he or she won't be so prone to jump on you.

Unfortunately, some of those pressure situations are not easy to avoid or change. Temptation seems inevitable.

Temptation is a voice in your head suggesting, "You're worthless. Why try?"

Temptation says, "If they treat you like that, you ought to treat them the same way. They deserve it."

Temptation says, "What difference does it make if you foul things one more time?"

Temptation works from inside, calling into question what

God says is true and scattering half-truths inside your mind. This is the most devastating aspect of temptation. Tempting objects and pressuring situations are not enough: they have to be accompanied by thoughts that operate inside your brain. Obviously you can't run from these. You can be tempted anywhere, anytime—in church, alone, in the wilderness (where, in fact, Jesus was most severely tempted). So how are you going to "avoid temptation"?

You can't really. Some people try to lock temptation out of their lives. They go only to "safe" parties and "safe" movies, and they have "safe" friends. They stay away from the beach and from non-Christian books, they build up a set of rules for themselves to follow rigidly so that temptation will never find a crack in their personalities. All these things may be appropriate at times in keeping the door to temptation closed. But any real solution has to deal with the brain as well. If you are free from temptation in your own thoughts, you can conquer the problems friends and things bring into your life.

I find an analogy helpful. Real, physical pressure is a lot like the pressure of temptation. You can "escape" it only to a point. Do you think a submarine, since it's water-tight, can go down as deep as it likes? It cannot. Even the atomic submarines built strongly enough to batter through the ice at the North Pole have a maximum depth. A submarine known as *Thresher* exceeded that depth some years ago. When the pressure became too great, the seawater crushed the sub's heavy steel bulkheads as if it were a plastic model. Searchers found only little pieces of that huge submarine. The tremendous weight of the sea had smashed its strong steel hull. That is pressure.

What if you want to go deeper, though, to reach the bottom of the sea? There are crafts built specially for that. They are strictly for research—steel balls lowered into the ocean on a cable. One researcher can just fit inside, shielded by the heavy steel armor. As he descends, he peers out through a thick glass plate, looking into the depths of the ocean to see what life may survive under such pressure.

He sees fish. You might expect these fish, living at such depth, to be built along the lines of an army tank. They are not. Where the little submarine has inches of steel to protect it, these fish have normal skin, a fraction of an inch thick. They swim freely and curiously about the craft. They sometimes flash neon lights. They have huge eyes. They are as exotic as any fish you will ever see. How can they survive under such pressure? They have a secret: equal and opposite pressure inside themselves.

In real life, some Christians deal with pressure by putting on inches of steel plate. They shield themselves from the outside world and strap themselves into a narrow space, peering out into the darkness. They are safe inside. But God's kind of freedom is more like the fish's. We keep our shape, not through steel plate, but by God's Spirit, who gives us inside strength to deal with each pressure point in our lives.

Romans 12:2, a noted passage of the Bible, essentially says this: "Don't be squeezed into the mold of this world, but be transformed by the renewing of your mind." Pressure from the outside wants to make you conform—to be just like everyone else. The Spirit of God counteracts that from the inside, through your mind.

It's no use telling yourself temptation doesn't exist. If you are on a diet, a piece of blueberry pie looks appealing, and there is nothing evil about that. I have heard people say that sin is really no fun, but that is not true. Sin is fun . . . for a while.

What makes temptation not fun in the long run are the things that come with it. You may enjoy a piece of pie today, but that means tomorrow you won't enjoy standing on the scales. You may enjoy self-pity today, but too many days of it will mean self-pity becomes *all* you will get to enjoy: you won't have any friends. Premarital sex may be enjoyable today, but what kind of attitudes and relationships are you building for tomorrow?

To change your mind, so it will have the strength to resist temptation, you need to appeal to higher loyalties, stronger desires. Resisting temptation is basically simple, if you think of it. It's a choice. You can look over the options and decide what you want to do. The problem is that temptation's pleasures are often more obvious and immediate than the

There is no more warming thought than, "When I'm dead, they're going to be really sorry that they treated me so badly."

Rohn Engh

pleasures of not giving in. Besides, your mind has been twisted again so you cannot always see clearly what is really good for you. It *does* seem better to be loved by your crowd of friends than to be loved by God. So you need to renew your mind—get in touch with what's really best for you.

You need to retrain your mind so that those rewards become as obvious, as the rewards you get for giving in to temptation. Perhaps these principles will help that process.

1. *Know what you're getting into.* Think about the long-term

The more you experience the joy God has for you in life,
the less appealing that old life seems.

results of how you act. Today it may be easier to fight with
your fiance' and get your own way. But what kind of
relationship are you building for the future? On the other
hand, what will obeying God lead to? If you can see the
attraction of the kind of life God wants to plant in you, you
will be less tempted to choose some other, short-term
pleasure. The Bible is full of commentary on how good God's
life is. Many of the Psalms speak of the sheer enjoyment of
being in touch with God, obedient to him, relishing the joys of
his world. Some of the Psalms also frankly confront the bitter
feelings that come when you see unbelievers happy and
successful without God, while your godliness seems unre-
warded. Read those Psalms and work on appreciating the
advantages of not giving in to temptation.

2. *Replace tempting thoughts with something better.* You can't
ignore temptation, but you can fill your thoughts with
something else. Often prayer helps—and not necessarily
prayer for help in resisting temptation. I often begin praying
for friends. Sometimes, too, when you are feeling tempted it
is very helpful to remind yourself of the power and love of
Jesus, who is on your side, who lives with you. Some people
use this verse to help them remember: "I can do all things
through Christ, who strengthens me" (Philippians 4:13).

But you don't have to fill your mind with religious
thoughts. Sometimes the best thing you can do is to pick up
an interesting book, call up a friend, or start working on a
project. If you are tempted to go to an x-rated movie, look for
another movie instead. The problem with many temptations
is that they are close and immediate. If you can put them off a
while and give your mind a chance to recover from its panic,
you will be in better shape to see the bigger picture.

3. *Your mind tends to follow patterns. Change the patterns,* and
you change your mind. In a family, kids are always fighting

over what TV programs to watch. They should change the pattern by figuring out ahead of time what shows they will watch and reach some compromise long before the tube is turned on.

For me, being tired often means getting depressed. I can lecture myself that I have no right to feel so sorry for myself. But a more effective solution is to go to bed when I am tired. Somehow that takes the drama out of resisting temptation. I outflank it instead of pacing the floor and praying for strength to resist it.

4. *Break the pattern of failure by confession.* When you go over your mistakes with another person, it changes your attitude. For one thing, you receive forgiveness, and your mind is put at rest. You don't get down on yourself and repeat your failures because of an "I-did-it-once, what-does-one-more-matter?" attitude. For another thing, a friend can help you to hold to your decision not to give in to temptation any more. He or she can check up on you, encourage you, and pray for you.

If, for instance, you have said something unkind about another person, admitting what you did and asking forgiveness from the person you gossiped to makes it far less likely you will ever want to do it again. You have confronted your sin in the open. You will remember that the next time you are tempted.

5. *Above all, remember who you are: a child of God,* loved by him. When tempting thoughts come, recall that fact to your mind: "I could act that way, but does that really bring honor to God? I want to be loyal and loving to him the way he is to me." The more you understand God's love, the more you will want to be close to him and obedient to him. Some of your temptations will simply vanish—they will begin to seem stupid. Their pleasures will be insignificant compared with the good things you are experiencing.

Reinforce this understanding of your own identity by reading the Bible and applying what it says by talking to God, by talking with friends, by listening to what pastors and other Christians say, and especially by worshiping and thanking God for what he has done for you. Christ's message is this: you simply don't have to act in the old way. You are a new person with a whole new way of acting. As much as God has loved you, how can you reject that love by ignoring what he says?

You get stronger every time you beat temptation. Each success is an exercise building you up. The more you experience what joy God has for you in life, the less appealing that old life seems. There will always be more temptations as long as you live on this earth. But the closer you come to God, the less you will want to disappoint him.

One more point: each of us has at least one area of special weakness. We may find temptation too strong there and experience repeated failures. Often we become discouraged and are tempted by a much worse sin: hopelessness.

At these times it is more important than ever to realize the limitless nature of God's forgiveness. It *is* limitless, which is hard for us to understand. But if you cling to it, someday you will understand. Not only that, but someday the area you are weakest in will be transformed into a special strength. ■

Competition:
"What is both
curious
and frightening
is that
the more
you win,
the more you need
to win."

—Bob Cousy

The Killer Instinct

by Philip Yancey

Image/Al Stephenson

■ "I walked into my hotel room and locked the door. For the next thirty-six hours, I stayed inside that locked room alone. I ordered all my meals sent up. I talked to no one. I didn't answer the telephone. I thought so long and so intensely about Frank Selvy that if he had walked into the room, I might have leaped at his throat and tried to strangle him. If anyone had touched me or even talked to me, I might have tried to kill him. Or, more likely, I would have broken down and wept."

Those words could be from a dangerous schizophrenic who ought to be strapped in a strait jacket. But they are not; they were written by Bob Cousy, one of pro basketball's all-time greatest players. Frank Selvy was his Los Angeles Laker opponent, and the frenzy Cousy described was his normal state of mind before a big game.

The next day, on the court, Cousy was watched by millions. His fluid, graceful body was a marvel of controlled coordination. Inside him, however, emotions were wound tight as steel wire, ready to uncoil with ferocious force. Cousy was known as a winner, and he had carefully cultivated what he calls "a killer instinct that impels you to keep going the extra mile needed to reach a goal when others slow down or stop."

Competition is so attractive, so omnipresent in America, that it's shocking just to hear a man like Cousy question it, as he did in his book *The Killer Instinct*. Because of competition, men have risen to great heights. Every four years the Olympic games demonstrate the beauty and skill that competition can inspire when the best performers in the world come together to test the limits of the human body.

I cannot imagine what a day would be like without competition. As soon as I step into a crowd, I am immediately aware of differences. I compare two girls' looks and decide which I prefer. I compare personalities and decide which person I want as my friend. I am conscious of how my clothes and my hairstyle fit into the group.

Yet it is easy for me to dismiss that kind of competition as trivial. Bob Cousy may have problem with the killer instinct, but my kind of competition is a normal, healthy part of life, I assure myself.

Back in high school, however, I was forced to confront the killer instinct that lurks inside me and everyone else. Every high school I have been in is a bubbling cauldron of competition. The moment I entered my school's doors, as a freshman, I was swept up in it.

Boiled down, I guess there were only two groups in my school—the Winners and the Losers. You could spot a Winner by the way he walked down the hall—confident, composed, surrounded by laughing admirers. Winners didn't worry if they walked over someone. The Losers were usually alone, using the halls like a pneumatic tube that sucked them into the anonymous security of a book and a desk in the next classroom.

Most of us weren't blessed with a body full of talents; we only had one or two. To become Winners we had to find our best ticket to success and exploit it. Those who were tough and sullen joined with the greasers and took on an indifferent, slightly impudent air. The strong and coordinated latched onto the whole swaggering *Sports Illustrated*/varsity letter/newspaper headlines world of jockdom.

The larger the school, the more colorful were the realms of Winners. Some had high-status science freaks, band freaks, and cheerleading freaks. In any case, the key to Winning was to find a niche and climb, often using other people as ladder rungs.

One incident in high school guaranteed my acceptance as a Winner. One fellow in my school, Hal, was a political nut. He

*Some schools have high-status science freaks, band freaks
and cheerleading freaks. In any case, the key to winning is
to find a niche and climb.*

breathed history, the Constitution, Congress, and all sorts of
relics that the rest of us thought we had long since outgrown.
By the time we were juniors, Hal knew he had no chance of
converting his classmates to taking politics seriously. So he
turned to the underclassmen.

Hal succeeded in reorganizing student government into a
senate and house of representatives, just like the real thing,
as he imagined. Each homeroom elected one representative;
each grade elected two senators. Hal was idealistic, perfectly
sincere, even fanatical. The underclassmen went wild, since

with homerooms they could control the house and pass all sorts of bills favoring them. We juniors and seniors were scornfully cynical.

Hal was also overweight, had a mousy voice, and wore baggy pants—a perfect target for abuse.

Because he was so fanatical and idealistic, a few friends and I decided to teach him a lesson. His political party had more than a thousand dues-paying members, mostly excitable underclassmen. We countered by forming a Student Rights Party with eight members.

The showdown came in spring. Hal with his armies had a newspaper, a platform, and a complete slate of candidates for every homeroom, senate, and student-body position. They even wanted a supreme court! And Hal—pudgy, bookworm Hal—was running for student-body president.

The Student Rights Party didn't bother with homeroom representative elections or underclassmen senate seats. We hand-picked the most popular kids from the upper classes (regardless of their abilities), signed them up with an appeal to their power instincts, and ran them for senate and student-body offices. A blitz campaign with screaming posters plastered everywhere, inflammatory speeches, and cartoon caricatures of Hal overwhelmed the school. We stayed up late at night creating slogans, and we spread untrue rumors about people. We also had a platform: Abolish the house and the mickey-mouse political parties, and restore cynicism to student government.

It worked. Our candidates won all positions except student-body secretary. And Hal was crushed. I was with him counting election returns, and as the trend became clear, he left the room, broken, in tears. His dream had been shattered, and we were triumphant. Hal never forgave me.

Student government did nothing that year, but I had become a Winner. The fact that sincere people were smashed in the process was just part of the competitive game.

My entry into student government had started out as a joke, a harmless way to poke fun at some fanatics who took school too seriously. But along the way my cynical friends and I had been caught up in the adrenalin of competition. We began to want to win. We stopped seeing Hal and his friends as sincere, respectable idealists. They became the enemy.

If anyone had forced us to think about what we were doing, in the middle of our campaign, we probably would have admitted we were wrong. But a taste for competition spreads like a disease. It soon possessed us so completely that all we thought about was winning, not the issues.

Really, it was just another form of prejudice. Humans like to choose some group—blacks, Polish people, rednecks—who are easy to scorn. It feeds our egos. It affirms to us that *our* group is the important one. We're the Winners, they're the Losers. Losers are always less than human in the Winners' minds.

Baseball players who are normally mild-mannered, devoted family men can become fist-swinging, cursing madmen in the pressure of a game. The next day, as they watch the reruns on TV, many of them must feel sheepish. *Why was I acting like that? Was that umpire's close call really important enough for me to lose my head in front of millions of fans?* Competition blinds us to that cool, distant perspective. It grabs us and squeezes until all we can think about is winning.

The same year as my Student Rights Party election, I became exposed to a man who, unlike me, seemed to prefer Losers to Winners. The man's approach was so novel to me that I couldn't stop thinking about it.

The man was Jesus. I read through the Gospels, and here is what I found: When Jesus met a Samaritan woman (the Jews' version of a "nigger"), he treated her respectfully and carried on an intelligent conversation, much to the annoyance of his status-conscious followers. When a hated tax collector named Zaccheus climbed a tree to see Jesus, he visited him for dinner that night. He even showed kindness to an adulteress, to people with leprosy . . . and to those who killed him. He said things like "Don't judge others!" and "Love your enemies."

At first Jesus' ideas turned me off, as did the Christians I had known. But gradually his love and warmth began to penetrate my steel defenses. He especially used two incidents to break through.

Athletes I knew were always wound up. They couldn't study,
they were snobbish and unfriendly, and even
the happiness of a championship season faded fast.

One occurred on a city bus which I rode each day to and from an office job. City buses often attract the washed-out and the destitute, the Losers of the world. This one was crammed with obese old ladies, sweating profusely, their stockings rolled down around their ankles. A middle-aged black lady, wearing tattered clothes and tugging a three-year-old behind her, stepped on and lurched down the aisle. Halfway back, the kid suddenly let go of his mother's hand, bent over, and *vomited*—right next to my seat! His mother cursed, grabbed his hand, and physically dragged him down the aisle.

I was repulsed. Why should I, in new clothes with a respectable job, have to smell stench and rub shoulders with sweaty poverty?

After moving to another seat for the rest of the trip, I thought about my reaction. I thought of Jesus—gossiped about for dining with prostitutes and sinners.

I also began to think of the misery of that woman's life. She rode this bus because she had no car. Perhaps her husband had abandoned her and her child. She probably wasn't trained for any job that made much money. Perhaps she was as repulsed by her slovenly appearance and sweltering life as I was. But she was trapped in it, with no escape.

I had labeled her "welfare leech" and shunned her the same way two characters in Jesus' Good Smaritan parable had shunned the bloodied victim in the ditch. I wondered how repulsive we—no, I—must sometimes look to God.

I left the bus sobered. Yet I had no solution. The women was pitiable, and pity was the kindest emotion I could work up for her.

Another incident took place in my college cafeteria. Tired of the usual mundane conversation with my group of

Winners, I chose a seat next to a sure Loser. She was skinny and shy and couldn't look at the person she was talking to. Though she was in two of my classes, I didn't even know her name. I sat by her quite by accident, but she seemed grateful. Making conversation, I started asking her questions about her family and interests.

For some reason, she opened up. She told me an incredible tale of a drunken father who would explode in violent rage at her mother and her. After school she would try to creep to her room without being seen. Fear and anxiety filled every evening. If she left, her father would be waiting for her with a belt when she returned. If she stayed, he might charge into her room unannounced at any moment.

I began to understand why she walked close to the edge of

How I Got To Be A Winner
by John Naber with Patricia Herbener

UNHAPPY SECRETS OF THE CHRISTIAN LIFE

the sidewalk, with her head down. Why she jumped nervously when teachers called on her. Why she usually sat alone during lunch.

It struck me that my own insecurities and fears—not really different from hers—were what had driven me to smash Hal and strive to become a Winner.

As I talked to her, I tried to build her up, to make her believe in herself.

And as I did I realized that both rejecting and pitying her would fail. Pitying was just an inverted form of competition: it, too, said, "I'm better than you." Somehow I needed to summon her true worth. But I did not know how.

I went home that night deeply moved by her story, but still troubled over Winning and Losing. I had been set back and

■ *In the 1976 summer Olympics at Montreal, a few faces emerged that the world of sports will not soon forget. One face in particular stands out, with its wide, mustachioed grin and big, friendly features topped off with a ridiculous-looking red-white-and-blue stocking cap. The face belongs to John Naber, holder of no less than four gold medals and one silver for his superb performance in the Montreal Olympics. Like any Olympic athlete, John lived and breathed competition.*

I remember one dual meet for USC when I tried again to close the gap on the world record. Balled into a crouched position at one end of the pool, I waited for the starter's gun. Almost before I heard the shot my nerves felt it and my body exploded, launching me like a torpedo into the race. I streaked forward, twisting, turning, pulling through the water. It was over quickly. As I touched the edge of the pool and heard the cheer go up from the crowd, I knew I had won. I whirled around to face the clock. My time was not good enough: I had lost my personal race against the clock.

I managed a sheepish grin and waved to the bleachers

was no longer sure of myself or of how to treat other people. I had fallen victim to the tendency of labeling people as Winners or Losers. How could I feel anything but pity for the girl in college or the lady on the bus? I thumbed through the Gospel of Matthew and noted again that Jesus had a lot to say about Winning and Losing. He said things like "What will it profit a man if he gains the whole world [Winning] and loses his soul?"

And I considered this passage: "Blessed are the poor in spirit, for theirs is the kingdom of heaven. Blessed are those who mourn, for they will be comforted. Blessed are the meek,

before heading for the showers. I had won the race: I should have been elated—but inside I felt as bad as if I had come in dead last.

As I dressed and started home I could feel the tension winding up inside me like a steel spring. I had felt this way before. The driving intensity of competition put so much pressure on me that I lost thirteen pounds at one meet and my face broke out in a rash at another.

I walked home slowly, mulling over the problem in my mind. What was going wrong? Dodging friends who would want to stop and talk, I thought about the C on my midterm test. Had I really done my best?

And what about getting turned down for a date for Saturday night? Athletes weren't supposed to have any trouble getting dates.

Soon I was feeling sorry for myself. *Oh, what's the use?* I thought. *Why should I knock myself out for 6 A.M. workouts when everyone else gets to sleep in? Why push myself until my muscles and lungs scream out in pain and exhaustion, and then still not make my predicted times? Why not forget the whole thing?*

By the time I reached the dorm, I was feeling so miserable I wanted to scream. I threw myself on the bed in my darkened, empty room. The frustrations welled up in a flood inside me, and the tears came.

I wiped at the tears with the back of my hand and reached

UNHAPPY SECRETS OF THE CHRISTIAN LIFE

for they will inherit the earth. Blessed are those who hunger and thirst for righteousness, for they will be filled. Blessed are the merciful, for they will be shown mercy. Blessed are the pure in heart, for they will see God. Blessed are the peacemakers, for they will be called sons of God. Blessed are those who are persecuted because of righteousness, for theirs is the kingdom of heaven. Blessed are you when people insult you, persecute you and falsely say all kinds of evil against you because of me" (Matthew 5:3-11).

In each instance, I could almost replace the words with "Happy are the Losers, for they shall be Winners." At first as I

for my guitar. As I picked and strummed a hopelessly melancholic song, my thoughts turned slowly to God.

I was setting goals for myself and doing my best to meet them, which was good. But I was neglecting to leave the results with God, letting him handle the rest.

Of course I knew that just because I was a Christian I did not automatically have all the answers to life's problems. But I did have Christ to help me. The tension spring began to unwind; I knew he would help me now if I would ask him. I started praying, turning all the pressures and frustrations over to him. I wanted to glorify him, not John Naber.

By the time I was done praying I had resolved for myself the fact that if I made the Olympics I would swim, not for the gold medal, but to do my best. I knew I didn't have to prove myself to anyone else or say, "Look at me, I'm the best!" I had confidence enough in myself and in my swimming that Jesus would love me - no matter how things turned out— win, lose, or draw. The pressure began to fade. Whatever happened in the next few months, if I only did my best and let God take care of the rest, I would be a winner.

It just so happens I excelled in a field that can be measured in terms of the *best*—that is the essence of sports. There may not be a way to measure the best student, the best son or daughter, the best businessman or parent. But if each day you strive for improvement in whatever you do, then you are a winner. ∎

read Jesus' list of people who were happy (or blessed), I thought he was just being patronizing. Since people were poor, persecuted, lowly, he was merely pronouncing a blessing on them, in the same way I might throw a bone to a mongrel dog.

But as I thought about it, a haunting question arose inside me. What if Jesus really meant it? What if all my schemes to compete, such as walking over Hal, thinking myself superior to poor people on the bus, driving for success, really were futile? Many of the most successful people were not happy, that was certain. Athletes I knew were always wound up; they couldn't study, they were snobbish and unfriendly, and even the happiness of a championship season faded fast. As former basketball star Bob Cousy said, the drive to win is never satisfied; it just makes you want to win more.

Jesus was the opposite. His values were not based on school offices or wealth or status or being cool. After all, he had no home, no money. He was deserted by his friends and executed by his countrymen. Yet he won somehow. He fulfilled his mission on earth. His life turned the world upside down, even though he never walked over someone to do it.

Perhaps the group of people Jesus praised could be true Winners because they had given up on competition. They were already convinced they couldn't buy happiness by showing off or succeeding. They were poor, downtrodden, defeated. As a result, they were more eager to accept God's love when he offered it to them. God's love seemed rather insignificant to me: who needed it? But to the people Jesus described, it would be a welcome, healing salve.

I began to agree with Jesus, admitting I had been wrong by living my life in one big competitive spiral. The apostle Peter (who constantly warred with egoism) once said, "Humble yourselves, therefore, under God's mighty hand, that he may lift you up in due time" (1 Peter 5:6). Eventually I humbled myself before God. I admitted I had been wrong in my selfishness and scorn of other people. I asked God to change my values somehow to make them like his.

As I was humbled before God he did give me worth—his worth. I found that fulfillment comes not from striving to be a Winner, but from allowing him to implant his goals and values in me.

None of the things my friends and I worried about mattered to God. Looks, intellect, strength, status, ability—they made no difference at all. How could we impress the Creator of the universe? Only one thing mattered: whether I gave myself to him and obeyed him. His way is hard, yet it is strangely fair: no one is excluded on the basis of talent or competition. We merely exclude ourselves by choosing against God.

I readily confess that my struggles with competition did not end that night. I doubt they will ever end. I still get depressed after a poorly played tennis match, and I know I will strive to do my best at my job. The difference is that earlier I was living for myself and I competed by beating out other people. I looked good only in contrast to them.

Now, however, the only audience that counts is God himself. I find that more and more often I am competing against myself, to do well, to please the One who gave me ability. The focus has shifted from other people to God.

Christian friends have helped the process. Most groups I had belonged to were ruled by status games. The best-looking, the funniest, and the smartest were given the most respect. But Christians operated more like a family. The moment I accepted Christ I belonged to this new family.

The experience was brand new. At school I was rated for everything I did. At work it was clear who gave the orders and who took them. But in this new family I mattered simply because I was a human being, and particularly one who acknowledged the all-importance of God.

Families are unlike anything else. In a family, a retarded child is just as loved and deemed important as a Rhodes scholar. No mother kicks her child out of the house because he has a bad case of acne (though many groups at school exclude him for that). Similarly, in God's family we were all equal before him.

As I invited Christ to transform me, I also found that with his love I, too, could see the beauty and worth of people around me. I saw Hal, the lady on the bus, the shy girl as complex creations of God. They didn't have to earn my respect: they had respect because God saw them as worthy. And more, I saw them as potential sons of God.

The climax to my search for God's view of Winning and Losing came when I found an amazing passage in the Bible: Ephesians 1 and 2. I read that passage and inserted the names of the most despicable, pitiable people I knew in the places which mention how God views us. They can be "holy and blameless in his sight," "gifts to God that he delights in . . . without a single fault . . . members of God's own family." It's what the good news is all about.

At first in my new life, I wondered if giving in to God would make me a cowering, defeated person. Actually it proved to be relaxing. I no longer had to go through life playing games, flexing my muscles in front of people. Now my attention began to focus on trying to show God through my life. The Bible says we can be like mirrors, reflecting the glory of God. Sometimes I feel like an awfully smudged and dirty mirror, and I wonder if people can see God in me. Yet, regardless of how I feel, this miracle has taken place. I don't have to prove myself any more. God has proven me and accepted me and loved me. I can live forever in God's love. ■

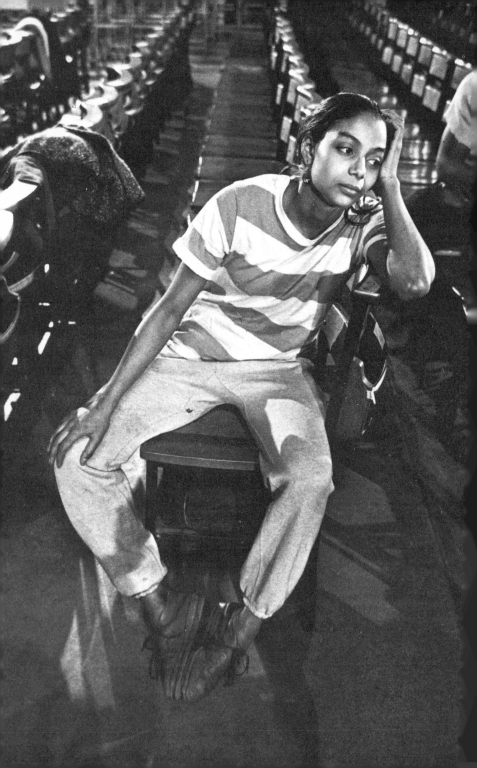

A Feeling Like Pain

by Tim Stafford

■ Kathy grew up in a church where she got the idea that God watched her like a hawk from heaven, counting up her sins. You could see by the way she walked and the way her eyes never met anyone else's that she was ashamed to be alive.

Then eventually, she came understand that Jesus was willing to take her just the way she was, to love her and heal her from all guiltiness. For a while she walked around feeling as though she had new running shoes: everything seemed lighter, happier, and freer.

Strangely, this sensation wore off. Her initial wonder at being accepted and loved grew old. Many of the patterns she had expected God to change hung on. She still did things she knew God didn't like, and she began feeling guilty again.

It did not help that Kathy went to a church where guilt was regularly hammered at her. When she read a chapter of the Bible that others found encouraging, she found every word aimed at her failures. A single word about sin was enough to bring on a week-long attack of guilt. She was just naturally sensitive, and after the initial relief of forgiveness had worn off, her Christianity seemed to make her guilt greater, not less.

A non-Christian psychologist, concluding that most of her problems were related to her faith, tried to "cure" her of that.

Guilt:
Let God, not your conscience,
be your guide.

Bob Combs

49

He did not believe in such a thing as guilt. He thought the best thing for everyone was to "feel good about himself." For Kathy, he certainly had a point: guilt paralyzed her. It kept her from serving others. She even began to question whether she really was a Christian.

It was difficult to argue with Kathy about her guilt. To her Christian friends, the sins bothering her didn't seem very great. They certainly had greater problems which didn't paralyze them with guilt. In fact, when they talked to her they felt uncomfortable: maybe they should feel as guilty as she did! They didn't know how to help Kathy. They could only listen to her while she spilled out her guilty feelings.

Kathy was certainly an extreme case but by no means unique. Most of us endure periods of life when we feel terribly guilty. Many psychologists would list guilt as one of the chief problems of their psychotic clients. Why is it that Christianity, which promises to forgive and heal guilt, sometimes seems to bring on more? This is particularly true for a relatively new Christian. He or she is on an emotional roller coaster for a while, and guilt is a major force pulling downward. Does anything cure guilt?

The instrument that tells you that you're guilty is usually called the conscience. It communicates through your emotions and warns you when there is a problem in your life.

It is very much like your body's pain-sensing system, only less reliable. When you cut your finger, the cut, dripping blood, is an indisputable fact. Anyone can see that it needs attention. But the pain that comes with the cut makes it urgent. This can be very annoying if you are doing something you want to do, like learning a new move on your skateboard. You would rather put off dealing with your cut. But pain won't let you.

Your conscience is designed to respond the same way to sin. If something is obviously wrong in your life, you need to deal with it. Guilty feelings force your attention onto the sore spot, making you drop everything else until you deal with it. It is God's way of making you feel the same way about sin that he feels about it.

But one huge problem comes up: your conscience is

unreliable. Your pain-sensing system is quite reliable: if you feel pain there is nearly always a cut to go with it. Yet imaginary pains do exist. Amputees sometimes receive terrible pain from a "phantom limb" that no longer exists.

This kind of mistake shows up much more often with your conscience. One person feels pain from premarital sex, and another doesn't. One person feels guilty because he stole from K-Mart, and another doesn't. One person feels guilty for going to a dance, while another wouldn't even think about it. The explanation is simple: God made your pain sensing system, but your conscience is largely man-made. We tend to think that our conscience is the voice of God, but it is really more the voice of our parents and our society, plus our experience, formed over many years.

There is a primitive tribe where all men are brought up to have homosexual relations with other men. There is a tribe where it is considered good to be a traitor to your friend. There is a tribe where lying is a virtue. All men, as Paul pointed out in Romans 1, *know* in basic ways the difference between right and wrong. But they don't necessarily *feel* the difference between right and wrong.

In other words, real guilt is not the same as guilty feelings. Some people who, like Kathy, are deeply bothered by guilty feelings are mostly plagued with false guilt. They have an oversensitive conscience which isn't tuned into the reality of God's teaching in the Bible. Someone needs to ask Kathy, "Is this real guilt or false?" Often people who have a bad self-image use false or imagined guilt to punish themselves.

A good sign of false guilt is that it is very hard to pin down. It often arises in response to "thought-life," to feelings and temptations. It seldom stems from a specific action that can be changed. If it is, the action is frequently one that is morally dubious—such as masturbation or dancing—or some action far in the past. I have noticed that chronically guilty people seldom fasten on something the Bible indisputably condemns or something possible to change. This leads me to think that false guilt is often a temptation sent by Satan, meant to divert us both from the wonderful sense of forgiveness that God means us to have and from the real problems in our lives that

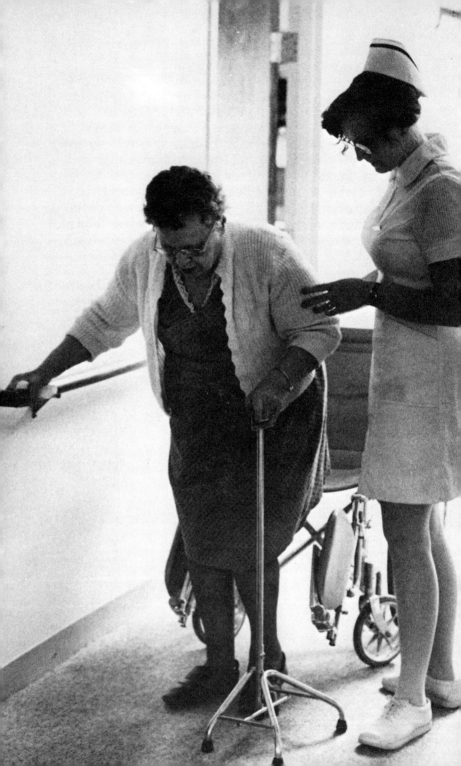

*"Let us stop loving with words or lips alone,
but let us love with actions and in truth."*

God wants to change. False guilt needs to be faced for exactly what it is. If you experience false guilt, don't pray to God (for the hundredth time) to forgive it. Instead, ask him to help you leave such self-hating feelings behind and get on with life.

In fact, this is just what 1 John 3:18-20 suggests: "Our love should not be just words and talk; it must be true love, which shows itself in action. This then, is how we will know that we belong to the truth. This is how our hearts will be comfortable in God's presence. *If our heart condemns us, we know that God is greater than our heart, and that he knows everything."* (TEV) Rather than being paralyzed by guilt, we are to get on with active love. There is no better reassurance of the reality of God's love in our lives.

You can adjust your conscience to reality—though it takes time—by confronting false guilt and by trying to absorb God's biblical standards of right and wrong. A good, accurate conscience is basically a shortcut. It helps you do what you ought to do without having to ponder your action. In a sense, a conscience is an automatic pilot. Your conscience will guide you through millions of choices each day without a thought. You don't have to think about whether to pay for the shirt you pick up at a department store. You don't have to ponder whether to accept what your father said about getting in on time. You don't have to wonder whether to cheat each time you take a test. Your conscience saves you the trouble. It lets you concentrate on more difficult choices.

But your conscience is not an infallible guide. It is not the voice of God. It is an emotional response that God has built into your brain. It can be, if you tune it properly, a helpful instrument pushing you to do the right thing. Left untuned, it can paralyze you or distract you from what is really important in God's sight.

So far we have been mostly considering what I call false guilt. What if your guilt is real? What do you do then? I can think of three possible responses.

One is to punish yourself. "I must be a terrible person. Oh, how guilty I am! How much God must feel hurt by me!" If you think of the analogy to pain, this would be like a person who, on cutting his finger, sits down in the road and begins to yowl, endlessly screaming how much it hurts. Little children do this, but adults should not. It is not a very good way to respond to pain—or to guilty feelings.

Another response is to deny the guilt exists at all. "Guilt is a neurotic impulse. It cripples and represses many wonderful people, and keeps them from enjoying life. Therefore I will never let myself feel guilty." This is like a person who makes up his mind he will totally ignore pain: "Pain is weakness. Only weak people feel pain. I'm tough, too tough for that." The macho act of ignoring pain turns you into a totally insensitive person. Ignoring guilt will also make you insensitive, and you will usually end up inflicting terrible (true) guilt on yourself, whether you feel that guilt or not.

A third response is to try to find out what is making you feel guilty and stop it. That is the right way to deal with pain. In fact, the whole point of pain is to grab your attention.

Finding the source of guilt may hurt. But in the long run it is what a good conscience is meant to do: make you pay attention to your wounds and heal them.

As a sophomore in college I went through one of the worst depressions of my life. (Interestingly, I don't always know I'm feeling guilty, I just know I'm feeling bad.) After a few days of real blackness, when I repeatedly cried out to God for help and seemed to get no answer, the idea occurred to me that I might be doing something wrong. Was there anything in my life that I knew quite well was wrong, but had been ignoring?

There was, as it turned out. I had been resenting a pastor of a nearby church. I had no good reason for my grudge: I just

Ed Wallowitch

When I was a sophomore in college
I went through one of the worst depressions of my life.

didn't like his style. I certainly could not see any connection between that grudge and the depression I was in. But I decided that I would try to do something about it. That week I went, somewhat painfully, to a Bible study the pastor was conducting. I decided I would keep going, whether I wanted to or not, and learn to love that man. My depression vanished. I believe to this day that at least part of my depression was caused by guilt—the guilt of holding a grudge, of cutting myself off from another Christian.

I do not mean to start anyone on a fit of groveling introspection. That is not healthy. I would say that if God doesn't show you quickly something you can change, your introspection should stop there. We can all find plenty of sins if we are willing to look hard enough, and some of us can even invent sins that don't exist. Don't do that. Just ask: Is there something that God wants me to do, something that I am ignoring? Is it clearly something God wants for me, something that other Christians would agree on? If so, do it. Don't pray long, weepy prayers for forgiveness. Change your behavior.

But you also need healing. When you have fallen down, you can make a decision not to run so carelessly any more, but you still have a scraped knee to deal with. Guilt also needs medicine: the medicine of God's forgiveness and care. Once again, 1 John helps: "If we confess our sins, he is faithful and

Giving In

name withheld

Bob Combs

UNHAPPY SECRETS OF THE CHRISTIAN LIFE

righteous to forgive us our sins and to cleanse us from all unrighteousness" (1 John 1:9). Let us not make this a big, soul-searching issue. It is as simple as it sounds. The only requirement is that confession be sincere: "God, I realize that I was wrong and you were right. I messed up, and I'm sorry. Will you forgive me and set me on the right track again?" That is *all* it takes, and John makes it clear that after such an action God will cleanse you from *all* your sinfulness. He doesn't clean you up 80 percent or begin a long process that

■ We all called him Tiny, even though he was a tall, muscular athlete. But he was gentle to me, gentler than any other guy I had dated.

The first month we went together, Tiny hardly touched me at all. But after a while he became more forward. We talked less. And he started handling me, unfastening my clothes. If I pushed him away even the slightest bit or tried to strike up a conversation, Tiny would act as if he had been wounded. He would sit up, draw his knees to his chin, and look straight ahead out over the North Carolina beach. The ride home would be silent.

I felt I was being stretched in two directions. At school Tiny was wonderfully kind. He would stick up for me in class. He would build me up, always complimenting my looks and consoling me if I got poor grades. Yet there was this one point of issue: I didn't *want* to give him my body. The tension was agonizing. Somehow Tiny made *me* feel guilty, as if I were the one hurting him.

Finally, after a few rounds of breaking up then going back together, I gave in. It was at our usual spot, a secluded corner of the beach right by a shallow bay.

I cannot describe the guilt I felt. Even now, remembering, I shiver. Why so much guilt? I don't know. Other friends of mine messed around all the time and thought it was great. But I was so miserable that I took a brief trip to my uncle's farm in Pennsylvania just to get away.

When I returned home, I was steeled to tell Tiny it was all

may take years. There, on the spot, he cleanses you.

I find an interesting discrepancy between the way most religious people deal with guilt and the way the Bible deals with it. We are preoccupied with all the shades of guilt. Preachers sometimes urge us to search for it in our hearts. We are to find it, confess it, and then go on to find more. Some people, poor souls, are tortured with a lot of guilt; other people lucky ones, feel very little guilt. If only the former could become more like the latter. Good news, we say: they

over: we couldn't see each other again. I tried to approach him several times in the hall, but each time he avoided me. The second day after I got back, I found this note shoved through the vents of my locker: "It was nice knowing you. Too bad things didn't work out. Tiny."

Several days later I heard a terrible rumor, that Tiny had started dating me on a dare. Friends told me some of the school jocks, knowing my straight reputation, had put him up to dating me to see if he could "take me." I do not know if it was true—it is hard to believe—but it certainly contributed to my feelings. I felt I had been used and tossed aside.

From then on, I would get a nauseous feeling whenever I saw one of the athletes in school. The memory haunted me everywhere I went; I couldn't shake it. I was convinced that was all any of them thought about when they saw me. Sometimes in class I would turn quickly and catch Tiny looking me over, and my body would go rigid. I knew he was remembering my body—and the game he had successfully played with me.

I became unbelievably jumpy. If a guy brushed against me in the hall or class, I would shrink back. If someone asked me for a date, I would make up any silly excuse to turn him down. I never went out.

In desperation I asked for an appointment with the Campus Life club director. I had to trust someone. Emotionally I just couldn't handle talking to my mother or any of my friends. I desperately needed some relief from the guilt.

The club director was extremely kind. His answer shocked

UNHAPPY SECRETS OF THE CHRISTIAN LIFE

can! If they work at it long enough they can produce a positive self-image, a deep emotional security in the fact that God loves them. Of course, they can also become better people, with less to feel guilty about!

True as this is, it is not the big picture the Bible draws. There you find no question of adding up columns of guilt to see how much progress you have made. It is plain: everyone has sinned and has fallen short of what God wants him or her to be. Then forgiveness comes with a bang. You were 100

me. "Tricia," he said, "before you became a Christian, you had reason for your guilt. You had fallen short of what God expects, and you knew it, though you knew little about God. But the fantastically freeing part of becoming a Christian is that your guilt can be dissolved. You have already accepted Christ. He died for the purpose of washing away that guilt."

I stopped crying and looked up, straight into his eyes. It was a new thought to me. Before, I had viewed Christians as the ones with all the rules who must be hung up about guilt. But what he was saying made sense: all of us feel guilt; but the Christian's guilt can be, in his words, smashed, obliterated, and forgotten.

"Here is my suggestion," he continued. "Whenever those memories return, don't ask God for forgiveness. Simply bow your head and say, 'Thank you, Lord, for forgiving me.'"

Then he read a verse to me: "If we confess our sins to him, he can be depended on to forgive us and to cleanse us from every wrong. And it is perfectly proper for God to do this for us, because Christ died to wash away our sins" (1 John 1:9).

"If you deny that," he said, "you are not trusting God."

That verse from the Bible is now printed on my bulletin board at home, inside my locker, inside my school notebook, and on the dashboard of my car.

I had the talk with my Campus Life director four weeks ago. The memories have returned, but each time I have turned to God and thanked him for forgiving me and making me pure in his eyes. It works: the guilt has disappeared. Praise God. ∎

percent guilty, and suddenly you are 100 percent not guilty. Full and utter forgiveness is free to anyone who wants it.

I think it is important to keep this Big Picture brilliant in our minds.

The small picture is our slow, individual advances. The Big Picture is the breath-taking advance that God offers us all in his son Jesus Christ. I think it is just what someone like Kathy needs to be told, again and again, until it gets through.

An old story captures this message better than anything I know. It tells about a man who has been involved in some sinful pattern for longer than he cares to think about. How many times has he confessed this miserable sin to God, promising that he would never do it again? And now here he is again, confessing the same thing: "Lord, I could die with shame. Again and again I have done this thing. I confess it to you, and promise that I will never, ever sin this way again. Will you forgive me?" From heaven come the words, "I forgive you. It is all forgotten. You are clean to start over again."

So the man feels wonderfully free. God has forgiven him. What more can he ask? All afternoon he revels in the belief that he will never fall into that same sin again. And then, that very night, temptation comes to him and he fails.

Well, he can hardly pray. Wasn't it just that morning he fervently promised God he would never sin that way again? He almost makes up his mind not to pray at all because he is so embarrassed. He will just ignore it, and maybe God won't notice. But his guilty conscience gets to him, and finally he begins to talk to God.

"God, I'm so embarrassed I can hardly talk to you. I did it again."

"Did what?"

"That sin. The one we talked about just this morning."

"That's funny. I don't remember any sin." ∎

Loneliness:
Is it a cruel trick
to keep us mired in self-pity?

The Magnet
by Philip Yancey

■ It creeps up on us, the dread disease of loneliness. When we become Christians, linking ourselves to a group of supposedly caring people and to God who is always with us, we assume that loneliness will stay away. It does not. It snakes inside us, filling us with doubts: *Do I really matter? Why doesn't Jesus solve my loneliness problems? Why doesn't anyone go out of the way to see me, to talk with me?*

Loneliness is not the same as aloneness. I know that, because loneliness seizes me most acutely when I am in a crowd. There, surrounded by laughing, self-assured people, I feel awkward and clumsy. I am afraid that anything I say will be ignored, or worse, I will be interrupted by someone with a more fascinating, winsome personality. So I retreat inside and head toward the corners of the room.

I have read books which categorize different types of loneliness, describe their symptoms, and offer practical suggestions to combat them. But those books always seem to miss the point. The descriptions are too clinical, too cold and scientific. An emotion as gripping and as universal as loneliness cannot be reduced to clever sentences on a page. Rather, when I think of loneliness, I see images of my friends who were lonely. Pained expressions are frozen on their faces. When I look closer, past the exaggerated memories into the person hiding inside . . . there I see myself.

In each of them is all of us. And so, to talk about loneliness, I must talk very personally and specifically about lonely people I have known.

Heather: Terminal Loneliness

Some of us can disguise our loneliness with plastic smiles and intense gazes into others' eyes. Not Heather. Loneliness was stamped all over her personality.

She had several strikes against her from the start. Because of a scalp infection, her hair came out in clumps when she brushed it. She would anxiously pull on it and more would come out. Her complexion wasn't the greatest. I knew Heather through her brother Mark, my tennis partner, who told me his sister would stand in front of the mirror for thirty minutes at a stretch, just staring and worrying.

Heather flunked a college speech class when she refused to stand in front of the class to talk. In most classes she would sit in the last row and spend her time doodling or leafing through magazines. She looked fatigued and pale, and a rumor spread that she had been taking some kind of drugs.

I tried to talk to Heather after playing tennis when we would sit on Mark's back porch, drinking iced tea. But whenever I asked Heather a question she gave one-word responses like "Yeh" or "Dunno." Carrying on a conversation like that was just too much work for me.

Heather soon got a job in a factory on the night shift and I rarely saw her. When I visited Mark, Heather was always in her bedroom, shades drawn, sleeping.

Heather's case is extreme, but really it is only an exaggeration of the most common type of loneliness. The great Christian counselor Paul Tournier said about himself, "As a child, I was terribly withdrawn. Orphaned quite young, I withdrew into my own lonely little world, even though I was treated kindly. My daydreams and secret projects only isolated me more from the others. . . . I felt I was of no importance to anyone and that no one was really interested in me."

Tournier pinpoints the root cause of this brand of loneliness: a poor view of self. In Heather's case the problems were poor skills at conversation and fears about her physical appearance. Even her friendly, outgoing brother Mark probably made her feel inferior by contrast. Other reasons for this feeling in someone could be a nagging parent, a speech defect, a failure to attract dates. In any case, a person starts wondering, *What's wrong with me? I don't seem to fit in. There must be something unlikable about me.* The natural reaction is to tunnel back inside, making it even harder for people to approach him or her.

The only cure for Heather or anyone else afflicted with loneliness is to relax those barriers a little, open up, and take some risks with other people. When I am lonely, I am afraid to show anyone else what I am really like for fear he or she will reject me. I think I need to show a confident, brash front for people to like me. But in reality, the opposite is true: people like to see someone honest and vulnerable. If I can ever muster up the courage to talk on a deep level with a friend, he almost always responds gratefully.

I wanted to be Heather's friend. But because she did not let me in on what was going on inside her—her tastes, her hobbies, her job, her favorite books and movies—we couldn't even carry on a conversation.

As I write that, I feel stabs of guilt because I think of all the times I have failed to open up to other people when I am lonely. Taking risks is hard, especially when you have been badly wounded by someone . . . and yet it is the only answer.

Paul Tournier ultimately found that there was only one source for the strength that would permit honesty and openness: God. When God's son Jesus was on earth, he seemed especially attracted to lonely people: tax collectors like Matthew and Zaccheus, fishermen who spent all day in boats away from others, a Samaritan woman shunned by decent people. He approached all those people with respect and told them they could be made whole by following him and experiencing God's love for themselves. God has the absolute right to tell us we are worthwhile, because he designed us even before we were born. Jesus proved how much he loved us by giving his life for us.

It is difficult for me to pick up a Bible and start reading when I am feeling lonely. I prefer to wallow in my loneliness. But whenever I do read the Bible I am reminded on every page how much God cares. He is there, and he is willing to meet us, if we let him. He can especially help with Heather's kind of loneliness, which comes from a poor self-image.

Christianity asks me to do a strange thing. Normally I like to boast about my strengths to everyone around me so they will be impressed. I instinctively hide away my weaknesses and failings so that I will look good among others. Jesus said that's all backward. I should learn humility, thinking about other people's strengths and not my own. And I should share my weaknesses and fears with him and with others. If I bottle them up, they will ferment inside me until they poison me. But if I release them, sharing openly with others, the cure is at hand.

Ralph: Imposed Loneliness

Ralph was not a predictably lonely person as Heather was. His reputation as the smartest science mind in my high school had earned everyone's respect. But one incident deeply affected Ralph, and I am not sure he has ever recovered. Each student was required to give an oral report in biology. While most of us slumped along with unintelligible explanations of photosynthesis and how birds know to migrate, Ralph took the assignment seriously. Though the report had a fifteen-minute time limit, Ralph was still going strong after half an hour. He had filled the board with an incredible maze of equations showing all the chemical changes that take place in the stomach during digestion: "Kreb's tricarboxylic-acid cycle" he proudly called it. When Ralph was nervous, his head wobbled back and forth as if his neck was not strong enough to hold it. His fingers began to work faster, and soon his writing disintegrated into a foreign-looking scrawl. Ralph's voice got higher and higher. He was excited, too excited to notice that none of us was interested.

Four guys including me were playing chess on squares drawn on 3 x 5 cards. Two girls were studying for a test. Some students were in various stages of dozing. And two guys in the back were tossing a soft rubber ball back and forth. Most of the rest were mocking Ralph's weird mannerisms.

Even the teacher was getting irritated with Ralph for consuming the entire class period. The more disinterested we looked, the harder Ralph tried to stir us. Finally, after forty-five minutes the teacher put a stop to his rave. "That's enough, Ralph," he said sharply. "I really think we must move on to something else."

For the next week Ralph wore a hangdog, dejected look. He took the rebuke as a major failure, and none of us went up to him to tell him we appreciated his effort. We avoided him, or joked, "Hey, Ralph, you ought to start a TV show called Mr. Science—at three o'clock in the morning!" We watched as Ralph lost interest in biology for the rest of that year.

As I reflect on Ralph, who became a very lonely person

Loneliness does not come from having nobody around you, but from being unable to communicate the things that seem important.

after that day, I think his loneliness was very different from others'. There were two parts to his loneliness. First, of course, was his superior intelligence and his interest in fields that bored or confused most people. Many bright people experience something similar. For example, the psychologist C. G. Jung confessed: "As a child I felt myself to be alone, and I am still, because I know things and must hint at things which others apparently know nothing of, and for the most part do not want to know. Loneliness comes not from having no people about one, but from being unable to communicate the things that seem important to oneself, or from holding certain views which others find inadmissible." Superior people can become misfits.

Yet there was a further, evil aspect to Ralph's loneliness: the part we all played in the classroom. Ralph didn't fit our ideal image of an aloof, casual student, so we quite consciously excluded him. Since he had ruined the class curve on tests, no one really pitied him. We forced our own standards on him.

You can see the results of this kind of imposed loneliness in any school. Athletes are okay. Joke-tellers are fine. Pretty girls are accepted. But ugly girls, shy people, fat people, clumsy people—they fight an uphill battle all their lives. Many of those people, like Ralph, have great things to contribute. A distant, intense personality is the thing research scientists and concert musicians are made from. Yet we cruelly stifle those trends.

My own role bothers me. Why did I help in the unspoken plot to exclude Ralph? Probably because there are some groups where I am not accepted, and I saw a chance to get even. I had never shared my interest in classical music or collecting butterflies with anyone in high school because of the reactions I knew my interests would bring.

For the Christian, there is no room for this kind of exclusion or imposed loneliness. Jesus came to break down barriers between people, between races and sexes, and even between personality types. It is obvious that God likes variety: he created animals as different as the ladybug and platypus, and he gave people startlingly unique looks and personalities. These differences, I believe, are given to us as a test. Do we have the maturity to accept people simply because they are God's creations?

The very quality of Ralph's strange interests could have been the basis for a deep friendship. C.S. Lewis pointed out in *The Four Loves* that friendships revolve around a unique interest that few people share. "Do you see the same truth?" he asks. One of us could have taken the time with Ralph to look for that glimmer of commonality which we shared.

Instead, we elected to ignore Ralph. I sometimes wonder whether our selfishness in imposing loneliness on him may have scared him off from an important career in cancer research.

Sharon: Aggressive Loneliness

On the surface Sharon seemed a very unlikely person to label lonely, because she usually clung to a cluster of people. When anyone told a joke, Sharon always giggled the loudest and longest. She was quick to gossip, and her emotions gushed out at high volume.

When a horror movie was showing, Sharon would talk for weeks about how *petrified* she'd been and how she just *had* to run from the room and get sick whenever she heard that *awful* soundtrack on the radio.

Everyone had his own favorite story about Sharon. The time she burped out loud in the library and was tossed out by Miss Trudeck. The time they were dissecting frogs in biology and Sharon went hysterical, then fainted. The time Sharon was sent home for wearing a "Linda Lovelace for President" T-shirt to school.

Sharon was great fun to joke about and tease, but no one took her seriously. No one really accepted her as a friend; she was always a tagalong, a mascot who obediently performed tricks for us . . . the school's dancing bear. No one suspected Sharon was desperately lonely. Nor did we suspect she was shrewd enough to sense that our joking with her was a thinly veiled mockery.

We never thought much about Sharon at all—until she went away. One girl insisted she had been sent to a home for mentally disturbed people in Texas. It was discovered that she had come from a broken home, and some said she had gone to Alabama to live with her father. Someone even started a vicious rumor that she had attempted a suicide ruse to get attention, but it had worked and she had died.

Even now, I do not know what actually happened to Sharon. I never thought of her as lonely until she was gone. Then it seemed the most obvious thing about her.

I have met many people who express their loneliness aggressively so that it becomes very hard to recognize as loneliness. Fat people who are always joshing about their weight, telling fat jokes. Old people who boisterously compare their operations: "I've suffered more than you have!" People who talk about themselves all the time. For me, these are the most difficult people to love. What I see on the outside, I want to condemn. I don't want to take the time to look inside and see people who are so frightened of life that they talk too loud and wear their fears like a neon sign flashing, "I need attention. I need attention."

A great model for handling an aggressively lonely person is Jesus' treatment of his follower Peter. Peter was big and blustery. He always stuck his nose where it didn't belong, made sure he got the credit when something good happened, and tried to come out on top in conversations. Yet Jesus could tell that many of Peter's words were a bluff. He rebuked Peter—sometimes harshly—more than any other disciple. He leveled with Peter and corrected him when he said something foolish. I have wondered what it would have been like if I had taken Sharon aside and expressed to her how she came across. I shiver just thinking about it, because I can visualize her exploding in a rage. And yet, that is what she needed: someone who took her seriously enough to help her see herself.

Even though Jesus corrected Peter, he also devoted time and attention to him and chose him for special projects, like going to the Garden of Gethsemane. And when Peter did something well, Jesus praised him.

At the end, when Jesus was crucified, Peter, his most outspoken friend, fell away. Asked if he knew the man he had once worshiped as God, Peter cursed and denied him. But a powerful scene recorded in the last chapter of the gospel of John shows how Jesus transformed Peter's loneliness. The disciples had withdrawn from their dreams of a kingdom and were back at their old jobs, fishing in the early morning fog.

Jesus approached, called the disciples over to him, and served breakfast on the beach. He asked Peter the same piercing question three times: "Peter, do you love me?" Imagine the pain Peter felt as he was forced to look into the eyes of the one he had betrayed. And, as Peter answered yes each time, Jesus responded, "Then feed my sheep."

Peter got the message. He was to quit feeling sorry for himself and get on with the task of reaching out to other people. He did so, and he became one of the most effective believers in history. By forcing him to confront himself, Jesus had prepared Peter to cure his loneliness by giving himself to others.

Peter's example shows, I think, that the solution to our longing is not a world without lonely people, but a world of people who use their loneliness to reach out to others. Every time we fail Jesus, he still asks, "Do you love me? If so, get on with the work of proving it by loving other people."

Roger: Deliberate Loneliness

Roger's loneliness was of a wholly different type. He was the first person I ever met who *chose* to be lonely. It happened one summer when he took a volunteer stint at a camp for the deaf, by a river in Wisconsin. No one else in the entire camp could hear; Roger got the job only because he had befriended a deaf girl on his block and had learned some sign language. (There was a CAUTION: DEAF CHILD sign on his street even though the girl was nineteen years old.)

When Roger returned from the four-week camp, the look in his limpid eyes revealed that he was different. He seemed as if he was always thinking of something else. After some prodding I found out what had changed him.

"I was the only one there who could speak well and hear," Roger said. "It was eerie—whenever I spoke they would look at my lips, not my eyes. I was the weird one in the camp.

Everything was designed for them. They had movies with subtitles—no sound. And at night they had a sign-language choir that would sing hymns by making motions in unison. They were so good that you could get the sense of a song like 'Amazing Grace' even if you knew no sign language."

Roger described those kids' relief at being together, away from normal people who could hear and talk. At the camp, no one avoided them because they stuttered or sounded funny. Roger said, "As the most abnormal person in the camp, I easily began to sense how lonely these people must be in our world. We make them feel like misfits. They never open up to others as they do with each other. I hadn't even noticed deaf people before."

After that summer, Roger went out of his way to find poor people and shy people and any people who felt left out. He rarely came to our office parties any more: "Too busy," he said. And Roger didn't smile so often, at least at us, his former friends. One friend put it rather cruelly, "If he wants to hang around weirdos all day, let him be a weirdo. Who needs him?"

I asked Roger if he knew what was happening. Did he realize he was slipping away from his old circle of friends? He assured me that he did. He told me it was painful and lonely for him to pull away like that, but that he had to make some choices. He had decided to spend his life with people who needed him.

Last I heard, Roger was working on a short-term project in Guatemala, helping rebuild a devastated mountain community. He knows very little Spanish, and I know he must be lonely. But somehow he has caught a vision that other people's needs can take priority over his own. Friends he left behind still get together in backyards to reminisce about good

John Chao

Last I heard, Roger was working on a short-term
project in Guatemala, helping rebuild a mountain community.

times but Roger is never with them.

I certainly would not call Roger unbalanced, or unfulfilled. I believe God meets his loneliness needs in deeper and more satisfying ways than those I normally know.

Sometimes, when I think of my friends Heather and Ralph and Roger and Sharon, I yearn for a world without loneliness. What would it be like if we were all self-confident? What if we did not need people to smile at us and notice us?

And as I fantasize I invariably come to a strange conclusion: thank you, God, for loneliness.

Loneliness is not the sort of feeling that normally evokes gratitude. There are no accurate statistics on it (e.g., 3,475,-212 people in America cried themselves to sleep last night because of loneliness), but it is safe to say that all of us feel lonely a good part of the time. Sometimes it goes away, when we are really connecting with friends, when we are loved, when our families are humming along as they are meant to. But always the gnawing returns. It eats away at us, depresses us, corrodes our self-images.

Why, then, am I thankful for loneliness? Because it is the one thing within me that forces me to reach out to other people.

I think again of my friends, Heather, Ralph, and Sharon. In their cases, loneliness had spread beyond the common cold stage; it was a cancer. They needed me. I saw it. Yet I thought, *Aha, I must be a better, more self-sufficient person than they are. I'm not that lonely, I don't need to stoop down and waste my time with groveling people who can't cope.*

If only I had been honest about my own loneliness, I might have been forced to them. Perhaps I would have been their cure, just as Roger had become the cure to those lonely deaf kids.

Loneliness is a magnet, just like sex. Even after the hairline has receded and the midriff bulge has slouched over the belt and the *Glamour* figure is a blurred memory—still sex magnetically pulls husband and wife together, to love each other. And so with loneliness. If we let it, it can be a magnet that impels us toward people, even when we're laughed at or excluded from a group or stabbed by sarcasm.

I have learned not to deny my loneliness by pretending it does not exist. It is, I believe, a normal part of life. The Gospels ring with stories that hint to me even Jesus felt loneliness. He was misunderstood and not appreciated. On twelve separate occasions, he moved away from a crowd of clamoring admirers to go to a quiet place of solitude. Even with his close friends—disciples who followed him wherever he went for years and listened to everything he said—he was lonely. If you read the accounts of the Last Supper, that heart-wrenching, emotional time right before Jesus' death, you can't help sensing Jesus' profound loneliness. He knew he was going to die, and he knew, too, that one of his disciples would turn him over to soldiers that night. As Jesus went out to pray, the disciples with him were so insensitive they kept falling asleep while waiting for him. They all deserted him as it became clear their master would be strung up and executed like a common criminal. Jesus faced death alone.

There is a tendency in each one of us to deny loneliness. We want to live life independently, not leaning on other people. But a nagging sense of loneliness keeps getting in the way. Sometimes it becomes so severe we can hardly think about anything else. I believe God created us incomplete, not as a cruel trick to edge us toward self-pity, but as an opportunity to edge us toward others with similar needs. His whole plan for us involves relationships with others: reaching out to the world around us in love. Loneliness, that painful twinge inside, *makes* us reach out.

What was the cure for Ralph, Sharon, and Heather? Perhaps I or any of my friends could have been part of the cure. And what was the cure for my own loneliness? Ironically, it could have been as simple as reaching out to Ralph, Sharon, and Heather. Roger found that his loneliness needs became less pressing as he gave himself to others.

Jesus summarized ethics in one statement: "Do unto others as you would like them to do to you." Applied to the problem of loneliness, that could be restated: "Assume everyone else in the world is at least as lonely as you, then act toward them as you would want them to act toward you." ■

Selfishness:
It spoils almost everything, including me.

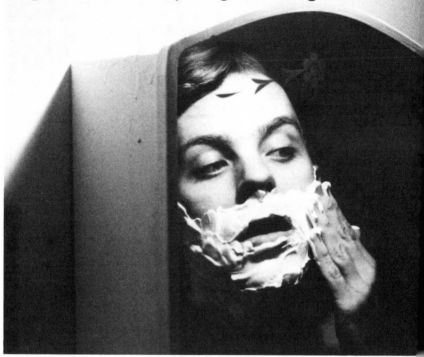

New Eyes
by Philip Yancey

■ How do I love me? Let me count the ways.

It starts with the sudden buzz of an alarm clock, this daily process of loving myself. I stagger to the bathroom, cup water in my hands, and splash my face, letting the water trickle between my fingers and dive off my chin into the sink.

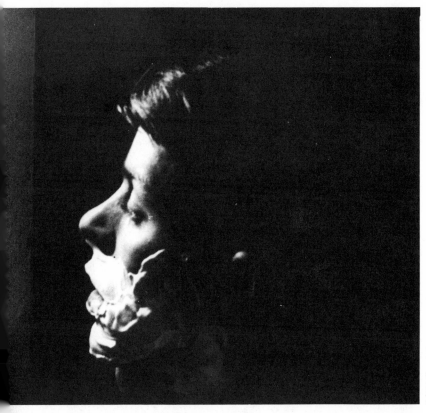

It takes me around thirty-five minutes each day to prepare for the world by showering, grooming, and dressing. That is two hundred hours a year I spend getting ready to impress people. During the day, walking through the hallways, I wonder whether I passed the test. Are my clothes right? Do people notice me? Do I fit in? Is my tan even?

Do people notice me? That is the main question. I certainly notice myself. It is as if I am the only person who really matters. To me the others are shadow people who scurry through vague, less-than-real lives.

How do I love me? I begin by thinking about myself every waking moment of the day. I am incurably selfish. My whole

*Whole groups of people can horribly pervert selfishness,
as when the Nazis determined that
their race had an exclusive right to the land of Germany.*

UNHAPPY SECRETS OF THE CHRISTIAN LIFE

life is a strung-together collection of movie scenes, with me at the center of each one, playing the lead.

The process started when I was a baby, I am sure. Back then, I really was the center of attention of my family. My name was chosen and wardrobe selected while I was still a mass of cells clutching to a hollow muscle inside my mother. Birth announcements went out celebrating the big event. For a while all my needs were met on demand. If I was hungry or thirsty, or just lonely, a sharp, piercing wail would bring instant attention. The world—my world—really did revolve around me.

I have a hunch that I am not the only one who has had trouble adjusting to a broader world where I am no longer the center of attention.

I can't stop thinking about myself. It even happens when I am within a group of others. When I meet someone suave and successful who attracts people with his good looks and smooth style, something inside me clicks. I start comparing him with myself, and if he is a threat I pick him apart, cut him down. *Who does he think he is?*

When I leave a party, my memories are of how I came across. Did I say the right things? Did I avoid looking foolish? And if I spent the evening as the center of attention—when it was my jokes people were laughing at—why, that's judged perfectly fair. I am always first to congratulate myself on any success, like an award or an article sold. It's okay for the spotlight to be trained on me; I just don't like someone else usurping my place.

I think I deserve my successes, yet I usually manage to explain away my mistakes. After I say something crude or miss an easy tennis shot or give a weak answer . . . even then, while on the outside I am hot with embarassment and anger, inside I am making excuses, rationalizing it away. *I was backed into a corner . . . The sun blinded me. . . . My teachers have no sense of justice.*

In these and hundreds of similar ways every day I confront my own selfishness. Some aspects of selfishness are natural and healthy. Psychologists call *self-consciousness* the phenomenon of constantly being aware of ourselves and how we fit in.

That quality distinguishes us as superior to other animals, many say. It allows activities like writing, in which we reflect on our own thoughts and experiences.

Yet, over the years selfishness has gotten a bad name, and with good reason. We have all met the person who never grew up. Like a 160-pound infant, he really continues to expect the world to revolve around him. He doesn't fit into a group because he always wants to go to his favorite movie, play his favorite game, and talk about his interests—no one else's.

Whole groups of people can push selfishness to its limits. The Nazis determined that their race had an exclusive right to the land of Germany. Refusing to recognize the value in Jewish people, they systematically began to exterminate them.

When Jesus came to earth, selfishness was one of his main topics of conversation. He sternly warned against it, always pointing his followers to the needs of others, not themselves. "The last shall be first," he said, "and the first, last."

The apostle Paul's great description of love excludes selfishness. "Love is patient, love is kind. It does not envy, it does not boast, it is not proud. It is not rude, it is not self-seeking, it is not easily angered, it keeps no record of wrongs. Love does not delight in evil but rejoices in the truth. It always protects, always trusts, always hopes, always perseveres" (1 Corinthians 13:4-7).

Despite what Jesus and Paul said, I still bump into this problem of selfishness every day. It happens that I'm the person in the world I know best, and I am the one I'm most concerned about. I feel as if God has set the ideal of unselfishness at the top of a steep ramp, and I'm on roller skates near the bottom of the incline. I have to skate hard just to stay where I am. Any progress toward unselfish love requires tremendous effort.

To complicate matters, much of Christianity can come across like selfishness. "Accept God and you will be happy," Christians say. "He will meet your needs." Christians can get a fat, self-contented look.

Painful, determined attempts to flush out my selfishness

usually end in failure. Brooding about selfishness is like trying to go to sleep. The more effort you use in thinking about going to sleep, the harder it is to relax and drift off. The act of concentrating on myself, reviewing all the selfish things I do, is merely one more way of focusing attention on me.

However, I have found one helpful clue which came after a very frightening revelation. It occurred to me: What if my brother, wife, my employees . . . everyone in the world . . . love themselves in the way I love myself? What if they gloss over their flaws and magnify their good points as I do? Could it be they consider themselves just as *important* as I consider myself?

The thought hit me suddenly that I had never considered for a moment what it would be like to be them. I had been too intent on loving myself to jump the gap and see the world through their eyes. Other people had been characters in my movie. But what about their movies, in which I play but a minor part: how do I look there?

I pulled out a telephone book and flipped through the three million names abbreviated in fine print. As always, when I turned to the Y section and saw my own name, it stood out as if underlined in red. How could I visualize those three million Chicagoans with their own families, personalities, and individual names? Each of those names must jump out at its owner as if underlined in red. That was unfathomable to me.

Finally, Jesus' words began to make sense to me. The second greatest commandment, he said, is to love your neighbor as you love yourself. I know Jesus didn't mean I should love my neighbor as much as I love myself; that's impossible, because I can't stop thinking about myself. And it encouraged me that Jesus didn't say, "Stop loving yourself so you can love your neighbor." Jesus understood human nature. He knew all people think about themselves and their own needs.

What Jesus meant, I think, is that I should love my neighbor *in the same way* that I love myself.

I know how I love myself. It is the main preoccupation of my life—my first thought in the morning, my last at night.

Jesus wants me to think about others. He wants me to praise their good traits just as wholeheartedly and enthusiastically as I congratulate myself for successes. He wants me to be as tolerant and kind and forgiving of them as I am of myself. In short, he wants me to act the way I would like people to act around me.

The idea sounded romantic until I began to think about some particular people around me. One young girl badly needed help. Her parents were getting a divorce, and there was a big question about which one would claim her. She was twenty pounds overweight and not too pretty. She acted sour on everything, so the few friends she used to have couldn't stand her any more. It was depressing just to be around her.

Another person, a fellow employee, was even harder to befriend because he was such a braggart. He seemed to need to impress everyone with his greatness. If you started talking about your job or your car, he would immediately butt in with an "Oh yeh, well mine's . . ."

Could I love these people as I love myself?

Another clue about loving others came from an unexpected source: the play *Man of La Mancha*. Don Quixote, the hero, is a tall, scrawny idealist who trots around Spain on his emaciated horse, playing knight three hundred years too late.

Quixote, the mad romantic, sees treasure everywhere when there is only trash. He spies Aldonza, a kitchen scullion, serving soup to a gang of ruffians, so he bows to kiss her chapped hand. "Sweet lady, fair virgin," he croons, "I have sought thee, sung thee, dreamed thee . . ."

Thinking he is mocking her, Aldonza angrily retorts, "My name is Aldonza, and I'm not any kind of lady. Look, look at me, slut that I am. I am no one! I'm nothing! I'm only Aldonza the whore."

Stubborn, persistent Quixote replies, "I see beauty. Purity. Now and forever you are Dulcinea, the sweet one."

All through Quixote's life he bumbles along, believing the best in people, encouraging them, being impressed by them. Summing up, a friend named Padre says, "He's either the wisest madman or the maddest wise man in the world." But at his deathbed, a long line of people whom he had touched came to pay respects. For in a strange, miraculous way he had made them into different men and women. By believing in them, he had taught them to believe in themselves.

Quixote illustrates that everything I say and do, even the way I look at someone (or don't look) goes into shaping him or her. I—yes, I—have the power to coax my friends/teachers/brother/employers toward seeing the beauty in themselves. Or I can help make them ugly, fearful, and sad—Because each day they are becoming a little more of what I let them know I think they are.

C.S. Lewis said it this way: "It is a serious thing to live in a society of possible gods and goddesses, to remember that the dullest and most uninteresting person you talk to may one day be a creature which, if you saw it now, you would be strongly tempted to worship, or else a horror and a corrup-

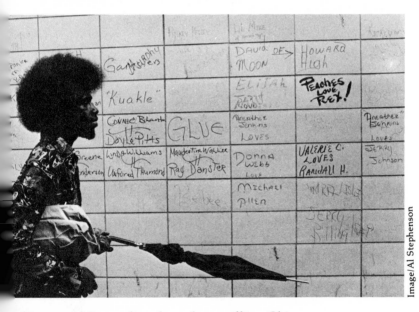

Image/Al Stephenson

How could I visualize those three million Chicagoans with their own families, personalities and individual names?

I Take Good Care of Myself
by Gary Sloan

David Strickler

tion such as you now meet, if at all, only in a nightmare. All day long we are, in some degree, helping each other to one or other of these destinations."

My own selfishness, if I let it control me, will assure that I will help other people toward the lower destination. Don Quixote was almost comically blind to people's true identity, and God doesn't call me to blindness. He just asks me to look through people's misery and distortion so I can see at the core what he sees: a unique human being of eternal value. That person meant so much to Christ that he died to transform him.

There is only one place I can get God's viewpoint—from

■ I take good care of myself, really good care. For instance, whenever I am hungry, I feed myself.

Whenever I am dirty, I wash myself. I brush my teeth, I clean my face, I wash my clothes, I wash and trim my hair, and I almost never forget to clean my fingernails.

Whenever I get hurt, I take care of myself. If it's a cut, I wrap a Band-Aid around it. If it is more serious, I go to someone who can help me. When I am sick, I take all kinds of medicine.

Whenever I am lonely, I usually spend time with my family or friends or someone else who understands me.

If I am thirsty, I usually drink some water or maybe even a soft drink or milk—just about anything that will quench my thirst.

Whenever I happen to be hot, I put on cool clothes, turn on the fan or air conditioner, or drink something nice and cold. If I am cold, I turn on the heat, or put on warm clothes, or drink something hot.

Sometimes I have questions. Then I pull out a book and find answers. Or maybe take some courses which will instruct me.

Whenever I am really tired, I go to bed.

Actually, I take pretty good care of myself; in a way, I love myself.

Jesus said, "Love your neighbor as you love yourself." ■

God. Only he can give me unselfish love to look at a seeming nobody and see the potential he gave that person.

There are four billion people in the world. How can they all be worthwhile and special to God? I can understand that only by concentrating on how much love and goodness God has lavished on me, just one of the four billion scattered from Alaska to Australia.

Jesus demonstrated that intimate, personal love by joining us on the earth. Paul said clearly, "Your attitude should be the same as that of Christ Jesus: Who, being in very nature God did not consider equality with God something to be grasped, but made himself nothing, taking the very nature of a servant, being made in human likeness. And being found in appearance as a man, he humbled himself and became obedient to death—even death on a cross!" (Philippians 2:5-8).

Jesus lived out a life of perfectly unselfish love. At Gethsemane, getting ready to die, he knew that on the surface this was a bad and painful trade: his life for the world. He was worth more than the world—who can count the Maker worth less than what he made? His pain and fear in the Garden showed he realized the stakes.

But He remembered that somehow his death was for the people he loved, and he trusted God to make the trade come out.

To love unselfishly, as Jesus loved, does not mean I discard my own needs and wants as if they didn't exist. That is impossible—I am always thinking of myself. It means, rather, to put two things above all others in my life: other people and God.

It does not mean that in looking for a friend I throw out my ideas of what kind of personality I enjoy being with. It does mean caring for every person who comes across my path, whether or not he or she meets my list of favorite traits.

It does not mean never having an opinion about where it would be fun to go with friends. It does mean paying attention to what other people want and need, willingly going to quieter places with those who are quiet. It even means going to a church service that in many ways is designed to meet the needs of people older than I am.

Unselfish love does not mean making the least of myself. It means making the most of someone else.

When I look at a person, I want to be aware of all the hurts and tensions he has endured by people calling him names, dumping on him in a crowd, excluding him from cliques. There is tenderness and mystery coiled within him, regardless of how placid he looks on the outside: the love his mother showed him as a child, the awards and recognition he got in school, the fears he hides from everyone in the world.

When I see a person, I want to borrow God's eyes. After all, *I am also a you*, and I want those who see me to view me that same way. ∎

Anger:
A match that can light a lamp,
or start a ravaging forest fire.

A Tightness in Your Chest

by Tim Stafford

■ I get angry. I don't mean I hit people or throw things. I mean that in annoying situations I get a boiling, tightened feeling that makes me want to mouth off. What's more, even when I don't lose control, it leaves me feeling bad. Sometimes I have to stew in my own juices for a while just to get over it.

Some Christians (not me) have a label for this: sin. They go farther, too: since Jesus takes away your sins, a Christian simply should never be angry. So it is not unusual for a young Christian to be tied in knots trying not to feel angry when, in fact, he is. You can become quite hypocritical, acting very calm and kind on the outside while steaming inside.

The Bible, however, does not call angry emotions sin. In fact, God is often said to be angry in the Bible, and so are his best followers. The problem with anger is not in the rush of feeling you get when something or someone crosses you, but in your response. What do you do when you are feeling angry?

I have tried to think about what situations inevitably stir up those angry feelings, and what my options for response are. I came up with three kinds of situations.

I had been standing in the college cafeteria line for about

five minutes. It took an unbelievable amount of time to get to the front. When I was nearly there, all of a sudden George, this big fraternity goon, put an elbow into my side and shoved in front of me.

"You don't mind if I crowd a little bit, do you?" he said, flashing an overly friendly leer. I was angry. I felt my face flush, and I had a tremendous impulse to shove him back.

This is where I get angry most easily—when someone violates my rights. Reviewing this kind of situation, I notice one thing: long before I decided how to react, and almost before I knew what was going on, I was angry. There was no point at which I could stop and say to myself, "Watch out or you'll get angry!" My body was angry before I knew what was happening—tensed muscles, boiling thoughts, and feeling were already there. I had no choice about whether to get angry. Where I did have a choice was in how to respond. Must my body's reactions run my life? No. I have found that I can make a choice on how to respond to my body and handle my angry feelings. And here are my options:

Option No. 1: Hit, push, or shove. Yell and make a big deal of it. This is a lousy option, since it usually hurts (depending somewhat on how big George is), can't be stopped once it is started, and tends to make permanent enemies.

Option No. 2: Ignore it. Pretend I didn't feel a thing. A slightly better alternative, but notice this: the angry feeling doesn't go away, it just goes underground. Sometimes I turn the anger on myself: "I'm a weakling. I've got no courage." More often it is turned subtly toward the other guy. I end up muttering to myself or a friend about George's lack of intelligence. The spitefulness doesn't make me look noble, nor does it help the situation. I still have that angry feeling.

Option No. 3: The soft answer. If I am ingenious, I may think fast enough to come up with the right thing to say. "A gentle answer turns away wrath" (Proverbs 15:1). Maybe I can make the incident into a joke (but not a joke at the expense of George—that's just another way of hitting at him). I can laugh and say, for instance, "Sure, get in front. I'm scared to eat what they're serving today anyway." Or I can appeal to George directly: "Hey, man, it's just cafeteria food. Nothing

*If I stifle the feeling, it may crop up again . . .
and again and again.*

Bob Combs

to get excited about." There is great room for creativity here, with a million potential responses that defuse the situation without ignoring it. A smile helps.

Of course, it will not always be easy. Sometimes people are determined to be obnoxious. It takes both sides to end a war. Sometimes I will just have to grin and bear it.

I was brushing my teeth (running a bit late—my fault) when my wife reminded me again I was supposed to take out the garbage. I can't explain why—maybe it was her tone of voice, or something I subconsciously thought I heard—but my hackles rose. I wanted to spit out some smart response . . . instead I ended up stalking out of the house.

In the cafeteria line I got angry because George violated my rights. But this time my rights weren't violated. My anger was unreasonable. Still, the feelings were there. What to do?

Option No. 1: Let my wife have it. Yell at her. I can give in to the impulse to make that smart remark, but it's not a very good idea. I will feel guilty knowing there is no way I can justify it, and it will start tension with her that will have to be resolved sooner or later.

Option No. 2: Stifle my feelings. This may not be a bad idea—after all, the anger is my problem, not hers. Trouble is, the feeling may crop up again . . . and again and again. Soon I may be unable to listen to my wife talk without feeling as if a dull saw is cutting across my backbone. There must be a better way.

Option No. 3: Think it out; talk it out. God has given me a lot to think about on how I ought to act. "Quarreling, harsh words and dislike of others should have no place in your lives. Instead, be kind to each other . . . " (Ephesians 4:31-32, *Living Bible*). So says God's Word. If I let that standard sit on my mind for a while, it will help my attitude improve.

"Look, I'm not prejudiced. I've had lots of Mexicans work for me. But I can tell you this: they don't know how to work. You can't afford to pay them decent wages, because they won't stick to a job."

My cousin said it when we were at his house. It really angered me, because he talks like that all the time. "Of course, I'm not prejudiced, but . . . " Yet he calls himself a Christian!

This incident is different from the first two: in this case I am not angry because of my own rights, but because of someone else's. I am justifiably angry. Alternatives for handling my feelings:

Option No. 1: Stand up and yell at my cousin. Rant self-righteously against prejudice. Seldom a helpful response. It tends to make conversations with my cousin a lot more difficult. Is my goal to make a scene or to change my cousin's mind?

Option No. 2: Don't say a thing. Pretend it didn't happen. A poor choice. My feelings don't go away just by ignoring them. I still resent my cousin inside, and any friendship I have with him becomes more and more superficial. I look down on him and complain behind his back. Or maybe I begin to hate myself for not having the courage to stand up to him.

Option No. 3: Make up my mind to talk to him. Maybe right now is not the time—but I can admit to myself I am angry, and plan to talk. I need to let him know how his comments make me feel, let him know they hurt. Maybe we can have a good discussion on what he is really saying. Or I can say, "Hey, you know I used to feel the same way until I read this book. It really changed my mind. Let me get it for you." When I make myself his ally, instead of his adversary, I stand a better chance of convincing him.

There are three things I have found I must watch out for. These principles apply in almost every situation that produces anger.

Don't deny that you are angry. God gave me my emotions, and they are good if handled properly. To pretend I don't feel anything when someone hurts me or takes advantage of me is to live in an unreal world and to deny what God has given. The Bible says, "In your anger do not sin" (Ephesians 4:26), so it must be possible to be angry without going against God. After all, God is described as being angry all through the Bible. If it is right for him, there must be times and ways in which it is right for me.

People end up with ulcers because they pretend nothing is bothering them and bottle up angry feelings. If I admit I feel angry, it releases the pressure. Then I can decide what is best to do.

Take your time in responding. My first response when someone hurts me is to hurt him back. It is unwise and un-Christlike. James wrote, "Be quick to listen, slow to speak, and slow to become angry" (1:19). The more time I have to form my reaction, the wiser that response is likely to be. The old advice of counting ten before blowing up isn't bad.

Don't nurse anger. Sometimes I take so long figuring out how to respond to my angry feelings that I never get around to responding at all. But Paul writes, "Don't let the sun go

down on your anger" (Ephesians 4:26). I can get days of sick pleasure from being angry at someone, but I'm a lot better off if I deal with the whole thing within the day.

I have concluded that anger doesn't have to be a bad thing. In fact, it can be good. Most things would never change if someone didn't get fed up.

But anger is powerful, easily mishandled, capable of great evil as well as great good. Like a match, anger can light a lamp or start a ravaging forest fire. What governs it is my will: my decision to run my body instead of letting it run me. God has given me control of this great power.

Learning control—not denying the existence of the feeling, but expressing it creatively—takes practice. Make your goal to defuse the situation and help other people, not to defend your own rights. God can make all of us like that; not sickly, pale Christians afraid of our own emotions, but fearless people filled with love for others and anger against pain and injustice. We can be people with anger under control. ∎

My first response when somebody hurts me
is to hurt him back.

Obeying:
We all like to give advice—
but who wants to take it?

Good Advice

by Tim Stafford

■ I am the sort of person who has plenty of good advice to share with others. I would be happy to advise you on everything from the best way to brush your teeth to whether the movie you liked was really any good.

But on a Sierra Nevada backpacking trip I ran into a problem. Three of my four companions were just as opinionated as I was. We had an unusually fine week of hiking, but it included a lot of bickering. If I selected a spot under the trees that would make a wonderful place to spend the night, Greg would quickly point out that we would not get much morning sun there, Harold would observe that it was far from the water, and Dave would say that we really ought to hike a few more miles before stopping.

Once we had set camp, each of use seemed to know exactly how much work he had done. If Dave suggested that it was Greg's turn to wash the dishes, Greg would quickly point out that he had already gathered firewood and started the fire. Any subject that came up—where to camp, what to cook, which way to hike—brought forth several confident opinions. I didn't think much about it. That's just the way it is when you hike with people like me. We love to give advice, and we hate to take it.

But a few days into the trip, camped beside a small ice-blue lake cradled in the arms of a high granite mountain, I began to notice something odd about Mark. He didn't fit. While the rest of us busily gave advice and formulated flawless arguments to prove how right we were, Mark had little to say. When he did make a suggestion, he made it quietly. Strangely, though, his suggestions were not followed by the sound of four jaws clicking into action with other opinions. He was met

97

by silence, or the rustle of people moving to do what he had suggested. Mark seemed to have a mysterious power: he could make us want to respond to what he said.

I thought long and hard, pondering what his power might be. It finally came to me. We responded to Mark without resentment because of the kind of person we knew he was. For one thing, he didn't give advice for the pleasure of feeling his tongue move. He thought about what he was going to say before he said it, and it seemed a pretty wise course to heed his suggestions. Why waste time discussing other options? Mark could be trusted to give good advice.

Of course, good advice is not always pleasant to hear. It is not fun to resume a standing position on feet tired from hiking all day so that you can set up a tent. No one leaps to wash the dishes in a freezing stream long after the sun has gone to bed. Yet somehow even Mark's unpleasant suggestions were easier to follow. That was because we knew that Mark would never suggest some job he wouldn't do himself. He simply never tried to get out of work. If a job turned out to be harder than we had anticipated, he would pitch in and help. He never left us stranded doing our "fair share" while he loafed around the campfire.

This thought brings me to God. For many new Christians, relating to God is fine as long as what they get from God is love and forgiveness. But then they go to church and find that some of the things they like to do are frowned on. They start reading the Bible and are confronted with orders on what to do with money, family, time, and any number of other things. Even in praying to God they get the definite impression there are parts of their lives that God wants to change. They are tempted to turn God off.

We who resent interference from parents or neighbors naturally don't want God's interference either. This is a major reason why some people will never listen to God. They think of the Bible as a two-thousand-page extension of the Ten Commandments, and they shut their minds to it.

Of course, the Bible actually has relatively few commandments: for every one there are pages of poetry, history, biography, or theology. But there is no getting around the fact that God has advice to give us on dozens of subjects, and he conveys it in the most dogmatic way possible. He says, "Do this or you will die." How dogmatic can you get?

God's advice, like Mark's is easier to take if you understand the kind of person God is. For one thing, his advice is not arbitrary. We listened to Mark because he was thoughtful and wise and didn't just toss up arbitrary opinions. If that made it easier to listen to Mark, why not God? He made the world you live in. He made you. No one understands your circumstances better than he does. If you can get his advice, why insist on figuring out everything for yourself?

And then, Mark was easier to listen to because he would never dodge the dirtiest job. God doesn't either. It would be hard to take advice from a God who sat in heaven, shielded from the terrible temptations and frustrations and suffering that can go along with being a human being. You can almost hear the protesting sneers, "He gives good advice, but can he take it himself?" The answer is that he can. God has not dodged the dirtiest job: in Jesus he came to face all our temptations and to die the cruelest death posible. Yet he took his own advice exactly and lived a perfect life. He doesn't demand of you what he would not or could not do himself.

You cannot get around the fact, though, that God's advice is terribly hard. He says, for instance, that I am supposed to love my neighbor the same way I love myself, forgive my brother endlessly, and never worry about where my next paycheck is coming from. How frustrating! Maybe Jesus could do it, but I cannot.

The Bible may not be two thousand pages of commandments, but the commandments are so hard it scarcely matters. If you take them seriously, how can you avoid ending up frustrated and bitter toward God? God can seem like a loveless parent with a list of chores that were supposed to be finished yesterday.

What makes the difference is this: like Mark, God does not hand me the list of chores and leave me to do them alone. He helps me. More than Mark (because he is much more powerful), God will make it possible for me to do them. Without his help, his commandments are impossible. Relying on him, I can begin to live as I should.

I would like to live up to what God expects. I would like to love my neighbor as much as I love myself. And given what kind of person God is, if he told me to do it I must now be able to, because he will help me with his infinite power to do what I cannot.

So his commandments can be read, not as harsh demands, but as promises. He says, "Don't worry about money." But the unwritten clause is, "I will provide for your needs. I will make it possible for you to relax and trust me." Wherever I read "You shall . . . " or "You shall not . . . ," I can also read, "You can . . . "

This does not mean that I am utterly delighted when I get advice from God. I am a stubborn person: I like to have things my way, without listening to anyone. But I have come to see that some people's advice is worth taking. It all depends on who is talking.

There is another problem that I have run into in my Christian life. Advice sometimes comes from ungodlike people—my parents, my teachers, my colleagues or my boss. It is one thing to take advice from God and quite another to take it from these faulty, frequently uptight people. Suppose a father has a bad day and demands that his son call off a date to help around the house—should he obey such an unreasonable demand?

Yet there are verses scattered through the Bible that make a parent's authority quite clear. "Children, obey your parents" (Colossians 3:20) There is also, "Everyone must submit himself to the governing authorities, for there is no authority except that which God has established" (Romans 13:1). God is a sensitive, all-knowing, helpful advice-giver. The authorities in life frequently are not. Sometimes they are obstinate, know nothing of what they are talking about, and give orders only to prove that they can make you do what they want. Why should you bow to the chip on their shoulders? Why take advice when you know it is not the best?

Before I answer that, I would like to make it clear exactly whom we are taking orders from. We are to respond to the

Though I'm a stubborn person, I've come to see
that some people's advice is worth taking.
It all depends on who is talking.

Rohn Engh

people who have been put in authority over us *while* they are
in authority over us. A student obeys a teacher while he is at
school, not because that person is an adult or even because he
is a teacher, but because teachers are in charge at school. If a
teacher tells a person to do something after school is over the
student does not have to obey. The student should respect
him, as he ought to respect everyone. But he is not under
obligation to obey.

The same goes for bosses. While you are working for them,
you obey. Should you quit, you don't have to obey at all. A
boss is not superior to you or even necessarily smarter or
more knowledgeable. He is just the boss. Someone has to be.

This is even true of parents. Some people stretch the
Scriptures to say you should always, all your life, obey your

parents. The Bible doesn't say that. It says, *"Children,* obey your parents." It tells everyone of all ages to respect and honor parents, but only children are commanded to obey. I take that to mean that as long as you are under their roof and living off their livelihood, you obey. But when the time comes for you to establish a life of your own, then you are not responsible to do what they say.

But why obey at all? I can think of four good reasons.

1. *In obeying authorities, you are obeying God.* God is the kind of advice-giver who makes advice easy to swallow. Here is one more piece of advice he has for you: obey those in authority over you. Sometimes you may not see why you should. Just remember that you are not obeying them because of how wonderful they are, but because God asks you to. You are

Jim Whitmer

Everybody has to learn to take orders—
from a teacher or a waitress, from a store clerk,
from a traffic cop, from the Internal Revenue Service.

deferring to his authority, not theirs. He is not asking you to do something that he was unwilling to do himself. (Jesus toed the line even though it meant the authorities killed him unjustly.) When your boss orders you to do something you consider unjust, it might help to think of it this way: if it's a careless order, that is for him and God to argue over. It is not your problem. You are to do what God has said.

2. *Someone has to give orders, or we would live in chaos.* Some of the time you will know more than the person giving the orders. (It is hoped this doesn't happen too often; most of the time, *in their area of authority*, the order-givers have more experience than you do.) But you can't hold parliamentary debate every time a decision has to be made. Someone has to decide. Someone has to oversee things and coordinate them. A teacher has to keep tabs on a whole classroom, not just on you. A parent has to think of the far-reaching consequences of a decision for every member of the family. A boss's job is to make sure everyone's work fits together. He may slight your work along the way, but it is hoped he has a better sense than you do of how your work relates to everyone else's. You may fry hamburgers better than anybody who ever lived, but if you are putting out more than the guys who wrap them can handle, it's your boss's job to slow you down.

Now, a boss or a parent or a teacher may fail to do a good job at coordinating everything. But how is he going to learn, except by trying? If you insist on anarchy, things will never improve.

3. *Everyone is under authority part of the time.* Authority is what makes things happen; it is the "clutch" of the driveshaft, and without it action would never get from the engine to the wheels. When you go to a restaurant, you are under the "authority" of the waitress. She sets the agenda, tells you where to sit, takes your money from you. If you tried to get up and get your order for yourself, she would tell you to sit down. She would be right. Everyone has to learn to take orders—from a waitress or a teacher, from a store clerk or a traffic cop, from the Internal Revenue Service.

4. *Authority usually protects a system that is worth saving.* I do not say obedience is easy. Sometimes you are placed under

the authority of someone who really grates. You can't respect the person, so what do you do? In the army, where authority is absolute, there is a saying: "If you can't salute the man, salute the uniform." You don't have to respect the person, but you should respect enough the position he holds not to tear it down.

Take the family as an example. I can't think of anything more crucial to our world than good families. If you don't think so, find some people who come from bad families or no family at all. They tend to have problems all their lives.

But suppose your father can really act like a tyrant. In the years before you grow up and leave for good, you have two choices. You can defy him, fight him every step of the way, correct every bad judgment he makes. As a result you

A Cartoon God   by JoAnn Read

Jim Whitmer

UNHAPPY SECRETS OF THE CHRISTIAN LIFE

probably won't have to do nearly so many unpleasant things. On the other hand, your "family" will hardly be a family any more. You will survive, but your family will not. You will merely be a collection of people living under one roof.

The other choice is to take literally Christ's advice that you "love your enemies"—in this case, your father. You decide to respect your father, not because he has earned respect, but because he is your father. Not only do you obey him, but you even try to act toward him as though he were a really good father. You ask his advice, get his opinion, and try to take him off the defensive. You salute the uniform, not the man; you treat him as the father he is not. You will survive—obedience will not kill you. Your family will survive, too. And the prospects are good that your father, once he is off the

■ Cartoons must have given me my first impressions of God: I imagined a haggard, hairy man with piercing eyes, wagging a long finger at me. Though he was obviously good, God seemed as distant and unapproachable as a stodgy old schoolteacher. He gave stern orders and expected obedience.

As a result, for a long time in high school I never turned to God with my problems. I would call Kathleen, my best friend, and pour out my story to her.

God seemed very removed from my hectic life of drill team practice, school bells, dating, and TV programs. I never could figure out how he fit in.

It was almost as if I would forget about God—as if I were holding a leash with a lion on the end and forget the lion was there. Probably I subconsciously wanted to forget because of all those cartoon images of a stern, foreboding God. It was amazing. Here I believed that God, the Creator of the universe, had chosen to be intimately involved in my life, and yet I could go several days without even thinking about him.

One day at school I learned from Kathleen that her dad was being transferred to another city. I was crushed. The defensive, will loosen up somewhat.

I think families are important, and that is why I would encourage kids not to settle for survival. We can think that all the problems we face, in families or outside them, are just the way things are meant to be. We can look at divorce statistics and say, "Marriage just doesn't work." We can look at the number of bad parents there are and say, "Family structures just don't work." But that is not quite accurate. They do not work easily—but they can work. With God's help, we can start turning back the tide of selfishness and sinfulness that makes authority so hard to live under. But if we give up on marriage or give up on families, we will have no raw material to work on.

People have two major concerns about taking advice from others. First, they worry about obeying something that is really wrong. After all, were not Hitler's henchmen just obeying orders when they murdered innocent Jews? Should

---

one person I confided in most would now be leaving me.

I reacted to the news like a child—with tears and anger. Who was I mad at? I'm not sure; I just felt a deep sense of loss. We had spent years building trust, so that we could talk about absolutely anything. I couldn't face seeing that friendship tear apart. I withdrew from other friends, turning down party invitations, and began pitying myself. Who could I possibly confide in?

A strange thing happened. With Kathleen gone, I began to turn to God. At first I approached him hesitantly, almost shyly. I would think about him while watching a TV show like "Welcome Back, Kotter." Could I trust him to care about the details in my life? I easily forgot about him: did God forget about me just as easily?

Somehow I felt better being honest with God. I found I didn't have to be on a mountain hike to communicate. I could talk to him in class, in my room—anywhere. He didn't seem like a stern schoolteacher at all; he seemed more like a friend.

The Psalms in the Bible encouraged me to open up with

UNHAPPY SECRETS OF THE CHRISTIAN LIFE

not they have thought for themselves?

Yes, they should have. But here is where Christians have a built-in advantage. Someone who doesn't believe in God either obeys other authority blindly trusting it, or trusts only himself, never taking anyone else's word for anything.

But a Christian can see that there is an innate limit to authority, because all authority comes from God. When Hitler stepped beyond the authority God had given him, Christians should have disobeyed.

There may be rare times in your life when someone, such as an employer, asks you to do something the Bible clearly says is wrong. It is your responsibility to oppose him and to encourage him to return to the kind of authority God has given him. You are not saying, "You're such a lousy boss that I'm now going to take over your job," but rather "I want you, if possible, to become the kind of authority God wants you to be." In the New Testament, the government was always

God. Psalmists bared their anger, their pain, their sour moods to God. In response he did not crush them with a heavy load of guilt or rebuke: he brought healing and comfort.

In the process of turning to God, I have learned something. I used to think my life was worthwhile only when it was filled with pleasant things. I surrounded myself with happy, loyal friends. I chose school activities I knew I would succeed in. In talking with my parents I avoided topics we would disagree on. Maybe that is why I shrank from the cartoon image of a stern God: I thought he wanted to take away my happiness and teach me "What's good for you."

As I experienced emotional pain, though—with losing Kathleen, struggling with my parents, and breaking up with my boyfriend—I was surprised by God's perspective. He didn't respond to my pain coldly; he comforted me as a loving father. He has promised to use anything in my life for good: to make me more like him. Often I can't figure out reasons why things happen, but I have learned to trust God regardless. That stern cartoon image is fading fast. ∎

respected. But when the government crossed over the line, refusing to allow Christians to tell about Jesus, they simply said, "That is not your right. You are in contradiction to God. Our first loyalty is to him."

The second worry people have is that, through obeying, one becomes a worm. This raises a serious question for me, because many people come out of their homes, schools, or jobs with personalities mashed into the color and consistency of oatmeal. God is not asking for this. He is not looking for someone who can't think for himself, who has no independence or spunk.

But authority does not, I believe, necessarily produce worms. In fact, I would guess that most people with strong, independent personalities developed their traits through the example of some strong, independent person who once had responsibility over them—perhaps a forceful mother, or a dynamic teacher. I would guess that most worms are produced, not by yielding to authority, but by a confused, unloving situation. When a family, a school, or a job are chaotic, when people get lost in the cracks, it robs people of the full personality God wants for them. Authority and discipline do not.

Read the Bible. Powerful personalities blaze through its pages—men and women whose lives changed history, who were afraid of nothing. Each model in the Bible is startlingly different, except for one similarity: they obeyed God. They lived under his authority. As a result, their strong personalities were strengthened, not weakened.

The Bible's model of obedience is a soldier trained for action. He is a strong person who has learned to work in the framework of an army, to accomplish things that could not otherwise be accomplished. That is the story of your life, if you are a Christian. You must first be strong: God lives in you, as a Christian, in order to make you strong. But then you are to harness that strength, being obedient to God's authority and working within the structure of families, jobs, government, and schools to focus that strength for some powerful good—to make a good family, to make a good school, to create a good place to work. ■

Doubt:
Broken faith, like broken bones,
can grow back stronger.

God

Bob Combs

Is There a
Who Cares?

by Tim Stafford

■ My doubts about God come most often in crowds. I stand still and watch streams of people flow by me. Each person is intent on his own direction and his own thoughts. Each, I think, knows and cares nothing about my belief that there is a God who cares. I feel lonely and insignificant, numbed by the democracy of unbelief. Who am I to say that my reasoning makes more sense than theirs? They look so solid and sure in their business: how could I ever convince them of a God who loves them? They aren't even interested. I wonder if it is I who am crazy.

Does it make you uncomfortable to know that I, who should be a sturdy, reliable believer, have doubts? That there have been nights when I literally screamed at God, pleading for some signal that he is real? There was a time when I felt threatened if a Christian told me of his own deep questions. If others as good as I thought of deserting the ship, was I only kidding myself to keep on believing?

Besides, I thought doubts were the worst danger to a Christian. I do not think so now. Doubts are serious. Sometimes they lead to a rejection of God. But more often, I think, if confronted honestly, they can lead to a stronger faith.

Other things worry me more.

It worries me when someone is knowingly disobeying God and rationalizing away his disobedience. Nothing will destroy faith sooner.

It worries me when someone pastes on a facade of vibrant faith, with doubts and loneliness lurking behind.

It worries me when a Christian can't get along with other Christians, but has a list as long as your arm of how he or she has been cheated, abused, and mistreated.

It worries me when someone is finding a "new, more mature" faith that finds unnecessary such things as knowing the Bible, praying, and worshiping with other Christians. An individual may abandon these things for a while, but I don't like to hear him saying that he has found a new, better state without them.

But doubts? They have their place, in the Bible at least. From the flaming questions of Job to the puzzled, stubborn "Show me" of Thomas, doubts are handled frankly. Doubters are brave enough to ask questions; pious people who know all the answers and quickly shut up questioners seem to anger God more.

When you are doubting God's existence, it may help to figure out just what is in doubt. Analyze your problem before you look for a solution. But do seek answers. The walls of Christian faith are not so thin that you will break holes in them by pushing too hard. If you ask honestly, you will find answers—though not always the answers you would have liked. "Seek and you shall find," Jesus promised. "Knock and it shall be opened to you." That was a promise to his disciples. They had chosen to follow him. Having done so, they heard the promise from Jesus himself, who founded the earth, that they would not remain puzzled forever, so long as they were willing to seek and ask.

Lonely doubts, I think, are the most common. I talked recently with a friend who had been going through a difficult time, doubting whether God exists or cares at all. But recently her thinking changed. "I realized," she said, "that I was really lonely. I knew all these people, but none of them really knew me. So I was angry with God, yelling at him that I didn't have any friends. That was the real source of my doubts."

It is hard to believe in God's love when there are no people around who love you. It takes unusual strength to live through such a period without severe doubts. We are meant to experience God's love through people, as well as through God himself.

But if you are lonely, make sure that is the focus of your doubts. Do not go on a philosophical tangent about those suffering in India. Speak to God about the reality of human friendship, and ask him to begin to show you how to make one good friend. Ask him, too, to show some purpose in your loneliness, some way you should grow through it. It won't happen overnight, but with a sense of direction your doubts about God will fade. He will become your ally in healing loneliness, rather than your antagonist.

Crisis doubts are often the most intense. Someone you love dies. Perhaps your best friend rejects you. Finals at school destroy you. Often during a crisis, you are very tired without even knowing it. The mental strain makes you need far more rest, and you often get no physical exercise. The pressure will not let up, and you are constantly nervous.

In *God and Man at Yale*, William F. Buckley said that whenever he had doubts about God he would lie down until he got over them. It is not so bad a prescription. Often doubts, and particularly crisis doubts, are a response to powerful feelings of sadness, fueled by fatigue. They will pass. Of course, crises can and should start questions that have lasting implications. But don't delude yourself by thinking that you can settle the meaning of the universe in one evening when you are low on sleep. You are not in any shape to do that. Recognize that you are in a crisis, ask your questions, but store them until later. Sleep if you can. Look to a friend for comfort. Often all it takes is a chance to express your doubts, and they fly away. If they do not, don't make any great decisions. Wait to resolve your questions later, when you are rested.

Intellectual doubts are actually, I believe, least common of all. The reason is that very few of us are intellectuals. But many of us wish that we were, and it is hard for us to admit that we cannot figure out all the answers for ourselves. So we phrase many of our doubts as intellectual questions, partly to keep at a distance our own loneliness and inadequacy.

There are, however, really good questions to be asked about the reality of Jesus Christ. If God is good, why is he willing to send some people to hell? How can we say that Christianity is better than Hinduism? Why do people suffer? If offering our lives to God really makes us new creatures, how come Christians often seem no better than anyone else? How can we put our trust in a book as unscientific as the Bible? There are many more.

I am not going to try to answer those questions here, though I believe there are good answers. We may not find final, once-for-all answers to our questions. But we will find answers that have satisfied men and women a great deal smarter and more learned than we. (A good starting place might be the writings of C.S. Lewis, particularly *Mere*

Reading about your faith may take some time, but since you are trying to decide whether your life as a Christian has any meaning, isn't the question worth some serious study?

Rohn Engh

IS THERE A GOD WHO CARES?

Christianity and *The Problem of Pain*.)

The saddest thing to me is that frequently those who ask these kinds of intellectual questions often decide the answer—and their whole life—on the basis of a few vague ideas floating around in their head, something a professor in college said with assurance, or the information in a couple of once-over-lightly textbooks. There is better information in any library or bookstore and, it is hoped, in any pastor's office.

If you are having intellectual doubts, follow them honestly to the end. Ask questions of people who are likely to have answers, and ask a number of people—don't settle for one or two. Ask for reading material. It may take some time, but since you are trying to decide whether your life as a Christian has any meaning, is not the question worth some serious study? If it is not—if you are content with the rummage sale of information in your brain already—then I doubt whether you are really being honest in your questions. If you give up your faith, you have cheated yourself. If you maintain your faith, you have cheated yourself too: these questions may come up again, or your faith may become superficial, afraid to confront difficult doubts and listen honestly to questions non-Christians are asking.

If you ask honestly and are willing to ask God for help, I think you will find answers that satisfy. That is what has happened to me, time and time again.

My doubt is more emotional than intellectual; I know that because it comes when I am tired. Still, it is real. I get weary of being different. Sometimes I would like to drop back into thinking what everyone else thinks. Instead of worrying about other people, instead of reading the Bible and praying and going to church, I would like just to think and do what *I* feel like. Being a Christian seems to be a tiresome ritual I'm caught in.

So what happens when I have these doubts? One thing that needs to happen, of course, is sleep. But there is more than that. My questions are not bad ones. What *is* the point of all these rituals we go through? Why *do* Christians act and think in such an odd way? I am forced back to the foundation of my faith. It comes down to this: if it were not for Jesus, I don't think I would be a Christian.

Now, isn't that an absurd sentence? If it weren't for Jesus, there would be *no* Christians. There would be no Christianity. But, obvious as the point is, it needs to be made. Jesus is who helps me survive when I am down.

Sometimes I think our version of Christianity could cruise along without Jesus. If someone somehow proved he never lived or never came back to life, we might get along just as well. We get rosy feelings from singing songs together. We make good friends through church or Christian groups. We have a point of view to look at the world from, and that breeds security. We talk about Jesus, but that seems to be a coded language for our good feelings. It doesn't attach to any real person—a person as definite as, say, my father. Could we substitute any other name for "Jesus" and, once we got comfortable with it, do just as well? Would "Buddha" do?

Suppose that someone lives Christianity just that way—strictly as a way of life, without really thinking of it as a relationship with Jesus, a real, living Person. I suspect the person might keep to the pattern all his life, enjoying being a Christian in the same way people enjoy being Republicans. Over the years he would grow to understand the system better—he would know how to argue over crucial points, where to find things in the Bible, and have theories about how a church should be run. But he would probably not grow kinder or more compassionate or closer to the source of life. He might spend his life confusing the good feelings he gets from praying in a group of friends with the reality of God. He might never know he had missed anything.

I think most people start with Christianity and only gradually grow to know Christ. We first are attracted by a group of people, a way of life, a leader or friend we trust.

That is my experience. I grew up in a fine Christian family. I have known some wonderful Christian leaders. I have been in some great churches, some exciting fellowships where things were really happening. But as good as all that is, it is not enough. You have to go beyond. Though some of the Christianity I have been around has been very good, long dry spells still came when my faith didn't mean much to me, or when I was without much support from other Christians.

But what I cannot get around, even when I'm unhappy, is the man known as Jesus. He is amazing. The more I learn about him, the more astonished I become. He is the ultimate answer to my doubts.

You have to read about him. In fact, there isn't any other completely reliable way to learn about him. Four pamphlets give reasonably detailed accounts of his life on earth, when his character took on a visible focus. It is no accident that the New Testament begins with them: Matthew, Mark, Luke, and John. They are basic.

What do I find in these four accounts of Jesus? I find layer after layer of meaning: simplicity I can understand the first time I read it, and richness the greatest of minds never exhausts. I find a convincing portrait of the only Man I would think it is worth dying to follow.

It is not just what he said. It is not just his ability to do amazing things. It is not just the way he loved people. It is not just his character under stress. It is not just his astonishing relationship with God. Incredibly, he combined all those things. He is unique; there is nothing and no one like him.

I could talk about many aspects of Jesus and why he appeals to me. But I will limit myself to telling you just one thing that always amazes me about him. Jesus is the only completely free man I have ever encountered.

I want so much to be free. I don't want to be imprisoned by anything. I want to soar as wildly as a hawk playing in the wind. In Jesus I see a model for what I want to become.

By "free" I do not mean free from all constriction or responsibility. People who have that kind of freedom are often tragically caught. Rock stars, with all the money and time they want to do what they like, sometimes commit suicide or strangle slowly on drugs. Some of the freest people seem to be those under intense pressure, like Aleksandr Solzhenitsyn or the apostle Paul in prison.

The freedom I am interested in starts inside a person. I figure we will always have some limits imposed from the outside. I am more concerned about the limits we have inside.

A really free person is able to laugh when others are bitter; he can be kind when others hate; he can be in a room full of gossip and not participate; he can be himself no matter what pressures are on him.

Jesus was free. Crowds adored him, but he did not fall for it and live to please them. Hundreds of sick people came to him to be healed, but he did not let that pressure keep him from priorities like spending time talking to God. The religious establishment criticized him, but he did not let that intimidate him, nor did he let it push him into becoming a stereotyped rebel. His best friends had ideas about how he should act and the kind of future he should expect, but he would not be influenced at all.

Jesus' freedom flowed from his identity as God's Son. He kept in contact; he remembered who he was in relation to God. The pressures could not mold him, because God did not

Jesus is the only completely free man I've ever encountered.

change in his love and his promise to keep him together. Even death could not take away who he was—and is.

For me, his most amazing display of freedom was in front of a rigged court that was obviously bent on murdering him. These were the religious people; they were also everything he had stood against. Now, in the ultimate display of perverted piousness they had him in their power. They didn't even have the courage to kill him outright: they had to try him on phony charges.

If you can imagine being accused of bribery in front of the Senate by the best-known cheat in Congress, you might have a hint of the mix of fury and fear natural to humankind.

Most of us have enough guilt stored up to feel we deserve punishment of some kind. When my car breaks down, I glumly, fatalistically accept it as something I deserve. But Jesus had done *nothing* wrong, not one thing in his whole life. He had never felt guilt.

So wouldn't you expect Jesus angrily to defend himself? Or to try to talk his way out of death? Or to beg?

He did not. At his trial he was repeatedly asked if he believed himself to be the Messiah, the Son of God. He was challenged to defend himself. He never did. Although some of the translations have wording that make it sound as though he did directly answer their questions, the actual words clearly indicate he replied only, "Those are your words." He did not defend or explain himself. Only Mark records that he once said he was the Messiah, the Son of God.

Why? In Luke 22:67-68 Jesus says why: "If I tell you, you will not believe me, and if I asked you, you would not answer." Even under threat of a grossly unfair, torturous death, Jesus remembered who he is. He knew they had the roles reversed: he is the judge of the world, and they were the ones who needed to defend themselves. They could play at mock trials, but he wasn't going to be caught in their game, to act out the part they imagined for him.

That was not arrogance. It was reality. The unreality was the trial, which tried to overrule the position God had given Jesus. He went to his death a perfectly free man, not only in that he could have called on legions of angels to rescue him, but also in the sense that he died without forgetting for an instant his personal security in God. Even on the cross, in horrible pain, he was himself. What did he do in those last, agonizing hours while he felt his body dying? He forgave a thief. He initiated a family relationship between his mother and John. He committed his life to God.

I can't get over that. When I read what happened I am astonished. I know that I have found contact with someone worth following. I conquer my doubts. Not only that, I give thanks for my doubts, for they have led me closer to Jesus himself.

Your doubts can often lead to a deeper understanding of God, for his answers will seldom be just the kind you were expecting. If your beliefs are shallow, then they will have to be dredged deeper. If the skeleton of your faith has grown crooked, bones may have to be broken before they can be reset. It will hurt. But don't be afraid: broken bones set stronger. ■

Prayer:
What happens
when God doesn't answer?

Stonewalled

by Philip Yancey

■ I have always been told that prayer is supposed to be a natural, spontaneous conversation between God and me. But too often in my experience it has become just one more frustration, mainly because of all my prayers that go unanswered.

I am not the only one with this problem. In fact, it is expressed beautifully in a novel that is required reading in many high school and college literature classes. *Of Human Bondage*, by Somerset Maugham, is mostly autobiographical. It includes a fictionalized incident that happened to Maugham from which his faith never recovered.

The main character, Philip, had just discovered the verse in Mark which says "Whatever you ask in my name, believing, you will receive it." He thought immediately of his clubfoot.

"He would be able to play football. His heart leaped as he saw himself running faster than any of the other boys. At the end of the Easter term there were the sports, and he would be able to go in for the races; he rather fancied himself over the hurdles. It would be splendid to be like everyone else, not to be stared at curiously by new boys who did not know about his deformity, nor at the baths in summer to need incredible precautions, while he was undressing, before he could hide his foot in the water.

"He prayed with all the power in his soul. No doubts assailed him. He was confident in the Word of God. And the night before he was to go back to school he went up to bed tremulous with excitement. There was snow on the ground, and Aunt Louisa had allowed herself the unaccustomed luxury of a fire in her bedroom, but in Philip's little room it was so cold that his fingers were numb, and he had great difficulty undoing his collar. His teeth chattered. The idea came to him that he must do something more than usual to

Tim Stafford

123

attract the attention of God, and he turned back the rug which was in front of his bed so that he could kneel on the bare boards, and then it struck him that his nightshirt was a softness that might displease his Maker, so he took it off and said his prayers naked. When he got into bed he was so cold that for some time he could not sleep, but when he did, it was so soundly that Mary Ann had to shake him when she brought in his hot water next morning. She talked to him while she drew the curtains, but he did not answer; he had remembered at once that this was the morning of the miracle. His heart was filled with joy and gratitude. His first instinct was to put down his hand and feel the foot which was whole now, but to do this seemed to doubt the goodness of God. He knew that his foot was well. But at last he made up his mind, and with the toes of his right foot he just touched his left. Then he passed his hand over it.

He limped downstairs just as Mary Ann was going into the dining room for prayers, and then he sat down to breakfast.

"'You're very quiet this morning, Philip,' said Aunt Louisa presently."

Almost everyone I know has had a similar experience. Despite prayer, best friends die in car accidents; friends and bosses refuse to see your viewpoint on a certain decision; you remain badgered by a petty sin.

The one survivor of a plane crash writes an article about how his prayers were answered, but what of all those who didn't live to write?

I have read the specific promises about prayer in the Bible and tried to follow the directions. I have wanted relief from a sore throat, or I have wanted to find an important paper which got lost. But nothing happened in response to my prayers. And so I wonder, Is anyone really listening? I must admit, this experience of unanswered prayer helped destroy my faith as a teenager for a while. If I couldn't count on God, who could I count on?

Cynical writers like Mark Twain and Bertrand Russell list unanswered prayer as one of the chief reasons they could never swallow Christianity.

The central problem with unanswered prayers is that Jesus

　　　　UNHAPPY SECRETS OF THE CHRISTIAN LIFE

Despite prayer, best friends die in traffic accidents;
parents refuse to see your viewpoint on a certain decision. . . .

STONEWALLED

seemed to promise there wouldn't be any. He could have said something like this: "Ladies and gentlemen, I would like to introduce to you the concept of prayer. Of course, you know that humans cannot be expected to have perfect wisdom, as God has, so there are limits to which of your prayers will be answered. Prayers will operate exactly like a suggestion box. Spell out your requests clearly to God, and I can guarantee that all requests will be carefully considered."

That kind of statement about prayer I can easily live with. But listen to what Jesus actually said:

"I tell you the truth, if you have faith and do not doubt . . . you can say to this mountain, 'Go, throw yourself into the sea,' and it will be done. If you believe, you will receive whatever you ask for in prayer" (Matthew 21:22).

"Again, I tell you that if two of you on earth agree about

Name-dropping

by Tom Bowers

David Strickler

UNHAPPY SECRETS OF THE CHRISTIAN LIFE

anything you ask for, it will be done for you by my Father in heaven" (Matthew 18:19).

"You may ask me for anything in my name and I will do it" (John 14:14).

Those are just a few of the strong statements in the New Testament. Others abound, such as John 16:23-27 and Mark 11:24. If you are interested, look them up. They prove to me that I can't squirm out of this sticky problem by saying "Jesus didn't really promise prayer would be answered." All those claims are lavishly made, in plain English. The Bible is not fuzzy on this issue.

So what is the solution to this problem of unanswered prayer? By studying each of the major sections of the Bible which contain the promises, I have learned some facts which help me understand the matter. The whole subject is still

■ "Tom, the governor needs a statement introducing our proposal for upgrading the state's law enforcement programs. Would you draft one?"

I was awed. Only six weeks earlier, at the end of my sophomore year in college, I had landed a job as a summer intern in public relations with the state in Lansing, Michigan.

I drafted the statement the governor wanted. That evening my director took my draft over to Gov. William Milliken. Late the next afternoon I found an excuse to leave the office and go down to the street-side newsstand.

As I rounded the corner of the stand, my eyes snapped wide open. There on the front page of the evening *Detroit News* was the announcement I had composed in my very own words, printed for all the world to see as a statement by Governor Milliken.

I wrote it. The governor put his name on it. Now people in Detroit and all across the state began responding to my words as if they were the governor's words.

In fact, they were. Once the governor accepted my draft and released it under his name, the statement became genuinely his, carrying his prestige and authority.

mysterious and slightly muddled, but my bitterness over unanswered prayer has faded as I have grown to understand some factors behind the role of prayer in the Christian life.

1. Jesus' statements, taken at face value, are impossible, so we have to search for a meaning behind them. Why are they impossible? Because people pray for contradictory requests, and God cannot answer both requests. In the Civil War godly men like Abraham Lincoln and Stonewall Jackson and Robert E. Lee all prayed for victory earnestly and frequently. But the North and South couldn't both win!

If Oral Roberts University plays Wheaton College in basketball, both teams might pray for victory. But I can guarantee that one team will not get the answer it prefers!

There is an even stronger illustration: Jesus did not get what he prayed for in Gethsemane. He asked God to please find some other way to spare him the pain, if it was his will (Luke 22:42). Often this basic fact is left out of Christian teaching on prayer. Our model for all of life, the perfect Man

---

After that first public announcement succeeded, I began to get more assignments for the governor. I never actually met with him—I just sat in my office cubicle two blocks from the state capitol and did my hunt-and-peck on an electric typewriter.

One day it hit me. I was writing a letter to a police chief which would probably go out on the governor's stationery with the governor's signature. The letter asked some questions and requested a response. I thought about that police chief reacting to my words as though they were the governor's.

All at once I realized how similar this is to prayer. Throughout my childhood I was taught to end each prayer with the words "In Jesus' name." When I grew older, I adopted what seemed to be the more adult form, something like "All these things we ask in your Son's name. Amen."

I always said those words, but that is all they were—words. It seemed to be the *correct* tag line for ending a prayer. Jesus told his disciples during the Last Supper,

---

UNHAPPY SECRETS OF THE CHRISTIAN LIFE

with perfect faith who taught us how to pray, was killed even though he asked God his Father to spare him! Obviously, some prayers get turned down no matter how faith-filled we are.

Paul had a similar problem, stemming from a physical ailment he called his "thorn in the flesh" (see 2 Corinthians 12:7-9). Despite three pleas to God to take the pain away, Paul's request was denied.

Therefore, I conclude that what Jesus said cannot be applied to all prayers at all times.

2. Each of Jesus' extreme statements about prayer was directed to a specific group of people: the disciples. During his time on earth Jesus selected twelve men to carry on his ministry after his death. These were special people, given special tasks by God (They were so select, that when the church decided what writings should be included in the New Testament, they included those written by the disciples almost automatically.)

on the night before he died: "I will do whatever you ask in my name." I had read those words before, and now I was getting an idea of what they really meant.

If I announce to the sky that some friend needs inner healing because of bitter loneliness, so what? My voice does no good, even if I shout. I need a representative before God, and Jesus is that person. It was the same way with the letter I was writing.

If I sent the letter with my signature, the chief would file it under "Throw away quick." Who is Tom the Sophomore Intern? But when the governor put his name at the bottom, the letter got fast response. It no longer mattered that the question originated from the head of an unknown student. The governor's name brought action.

When we say "In Jesus' name," Jesus himself promises to put all the power and authority of his name behind our puny words. It is not a magical phrase at all. It is just a fantastic promise from one who has the authority of God. ∎

Could it be that Jesus gave his disciples certain rights and privileges in prayer which don't apply to all Christians in the same degree? After all, who of us can duplicate Peter's miracles or John's inspired writings?

The Gospel writers do not explicitly say, "These commands apply to the disciples only," but they do tell us, in each case, that Jesus was talking to his twelve disciples, not a large crowd.

Frankly, I don't know how far to carry this point. But perhaps it could help explain the sweeping nature of Jesus' promises. *Perhaps* he was investing in the disciples a specific gift of boldness and insight into God's will. They were mature men who had spent three years learning directly from Jesus; chances are they would have a good idea of which prayers would further God's purpose on earth and which would be capricious (of the "help our team win" category).

Interestingly, in such passages as 1 John 5:14-15, John, writing to a large group, carefully says that "if we ask anything according to his will, he hears us." That phrase "according to his will" is a key to truth.

3. Since it was Jesus who made the sweeping claims about prayer, I looked carefully at the kind of prayers he prayed. One trend surprised me. I had always viewed prayers as an act focused on and determined by me, the pray-er. But Jesus' prayers showed that really the focus is on the Father, the One prayed to. He used prayer as a time to commune with the Father, to refresh himself in God's will, to ask for strength. He also used it to thank God for the world and to mention his friends who had needs. It was a conversation, not a shopping list.

Charlie Shedd calls prayer "an inner dialogue with your best friend." I began to see that I had instead viewed it as a magic wand I could wave to make God do what I want. I am not the one in charge of prayer, however; God is.

Many people share the misconception I once had about prayer. For example, Mark Twain, who was bothered by unanswered prayer, expressed the dilemma in *Huckleberry Finn*. Huck got a lesson from Miss Watson in prayer.

"She told me to pray every day, and whatever I asked for I

UNHAPPY SECRETS OF THE CHRISTIAN LIFE

I was surprised to find that requests are a small part of prayer.
Some prayer is worship, some repentance, some praise.

would get it. But it warn't so. I tried it. Once I got a fishline but no hooks. It warn't any good to me without hooks. I tried for the hooks three or four times, but somehow I couldn't make it work. By and by one day I asked Miss Watson to try for me, but she said I was a fool. She never told me why. I couldn't make it out no way.

"I set down one time back in the woods and had a long think about it. I says to myself, 'If a body can get anything they pray for, why don't Deacon Winn get back the money he lost on pork? Why don't the widow get back her silver snuffbox that was stolen? Why can't Miss Watson fat up? No! says I to myself, there ain't nothing in it."

Obviously, Huck wanted a genie in a bottle who would perform his wishes on command, not a God who would be Lord of his life. Faith, to him, was a mental flex to get what he wanted. But faith should be in God, trusting his love and willingness to respond wisely.

As I went through the Bible examining prayers, I couldn't help noticing that requests are a small part of prayer. Some prayer is worship, some repentance, some praise. The Psalms, for example, are a series of prayers set to poetry. Read through them and notice how few of them are essentially request prayers.

The prayers which are requests are simply that: *requests.* Prayer is not a vending machine which spits out the appropriate reward. It is a call to a loving Father to relate to us.

The motive of prayer cannot be "What can I get?" That's magic. It has to be, "God, I believe this is your will, but it's beyond my power. Can you help me?" In the Lord's Prayer, Jesus expressed it this way: "Thy kingdom come, thy will be done."

The Bible is clear that God hears our prayers, even the ones which don't get answered as we would like. He carefully considers the most absurd and selfish requests. When children ask foolish things of wise parents—such as, "May I stay up to watch the late, late show?" or "Will you let me drive even though I'm only twelve?"—they don't always get their way. Often the parents know better what is good for the child.

While studying the types of request prayers which are illustrated in the Bible, I noticed that even their styles differ greatly. I observe at least three kinds:

1. The humble, submissive-to-the-will-of-God request as Jesus prayed in Gethsemane before he was crucified. That prayer takes deep trust in God, because we are actually saying "I honestly want to do what you want me to do." In Jesus' case, that meant being put to death. These prayers usually have the tag, "If it be your will," and in fact some Christians believe it is proper to pray all prayers with that attitude.

2. The unusual prayers made by people with simple faith who really believe God will honor them. Often young Christians have the most beautiful faith. Experienced, more sophisticated Christians sometimes scorn outlandish requests like healing, radical changes, huge amounts of money. And they have a point: taken to its extreme this type of faith can result in tragedy. Every so often newspapers carry stories of religious parents whose children die after they refuse to let them be treated for leukemia. (Remember Somerset Maugham, who lost his faith because he gambled on a miracle.) Yet, if you study the Bible, it is clear there is a place for childlike, bold faith. Jesus praised such faith, as in the centurion (Luke 7). Many of his parables about prayer encouraged audacious requests.

These prayers puzzle me. Why do some people's prayers get answered with regularity, while mine sputter along? At various times in my Christian life I have thought of prayer as a spiritual muscle. I saw faith as similar to doing push-ups: if you work hard and do them every day, soon you will get the reward of a bulging arm and have more strength to do what you want.

But prayer doesn't work quite that way. Faith is not something I can muster up by concentrating hard, like a yoga meditation. I know that, because some of the most spectacular answers to prayer I have seen occur to brand-new Christians who are "just ignorant and naive enough" to believe that God really will perform a miracle for them. God seems to honor that enthusiastic young faith.

3. The large requests made when you are praying for something you are almost sure is the will of God. Thus Jesus and his followers could pray with complete confidence for physical healing, because they were so in touch with God they knew it to be his will. This last category seems to me to be the goal for mature Christians, but I find most of my request prayers fall into the first category.

Regardless of how we categorize prayers, we cannot take Scripture verses and try to make a money-back guarantee that God will answer any prayer. For us to pray with confidence, we should have good reasons to believe the answer we want is closely aligned with God's will.

God's will is complex and harder to understand. He is concerned, not only for us personally, but for the whole universe. Charlie Shedd expresses it this way: "Our great, wonderful, loving God has answers we don't know anything about. This is where faith comes in. We have to believe that he means it when he says, 'Our lives are eternal. What you see happening here is just the backside of the rug. It isn't so beautiful on this side as it is on the finished side. You have to believe me that under all the circumstances, I know what's best.' About a thousand years from now you will probably say, 'Hey, I see!'"

Paul said, "And we know that in all things God works for the good of those who love him, who have been called according to his purpose" (Romans 8:28). Joni Eareckson experienced this phenomenon after a diving accident left her paralyzed. Her prayers for healing were not answered, but God is using her life-story in books and a movie to encourage the faith of millions. Her pain did work out for the cause of good.

An enormous warfare between good and evil is raging around us and in us. Prayer offers a few minutes for us to loudly show we are on the side of good. We are linked up with God's concerns and God's will. We make contact with our King.

Faith is not a formula to unlock God's well-kept secret. It is a trust in God, whether he does things I want or lets me endure hard times. In Hebrews 11, sometimes called the

"Faith Hall of Fame," some of the giants of the faith hardly got the results they wanted. Some were rescued from floods and Pharaohs and lions. But right along with them were others who were beaten to death, lashed with whips, or sawed in two.

Both groups had powerful faith which is hailed as a model for us. Faith didn't necessarily remove the problems, but it won God's praise and reward. Faith is not an inflatable quantity you can pump up to get God's attention. It is a quality of trust that takes us outside ourselves into God's desires on earth.

Often, when it looks as if one of my requests has been turned down, God answers it indirectly. Another who experienced this is the mother of Augustine. She prayed all night that God would stop her son from going to Italy, because she wanted him to become a Christian. While she was praying, he sailed away, and it seemed her prayers went unheard. But in Italy Augustine was converted, and he became a great Christian leader. God is loving and wise, and he can deny our prayers in order to bring even greater blessing to us.

Discussions on prayer tend to get complex and confusing. Perhaps that is why the Bible doesn't outline the process in detail, showing us all the fine points and mysteries of prayer. Rather, we are beckoned to come to God in prayer as a child, setting aside our doubts. Why did Jesus use such extravagant promises? I don't fully know. Maybe it was to push us toward extravagant faith.

Jesus said, "Which of you fathers, if your son asks for a fish, will give him a snake instead? Or if he asks for an egg, will give him a scorpion? If you then, though you are evil, know how to give good gifts to your children, how much more will your Father in Heaven give the Holy Spirit to those who ask him!" (Luke 11:11-13).

To me, it is not so amazing that God chooses to deny some of our requests. What is amazing is that we are listened to at all! Every prayer ends up in God's active file. Our role is to flood him with requests and then commit to him the trust that accepts his answers. ∎

Legalism:
It's easy to spot in someone else,
hard to avoid in yourself.

A Perfect,
Empty Shell

by Philip Yancey

■ Jesus Christ knew various crooked people when he was on earth: sneaky tax collectors, streetwalkers, thieves, ruthless soldiers. But as he traveled the streets of Jerusalem and other Jewish towns, one group particularly seemed to get under his skin. He singled them out for his strongest attacks. "Snakes!"

he called them. "Tangle of vipers! Fools! Hypocrites! Blind guides! Whitewashed tombs!"

Strangely, the people who made Jesus livid with anger were the ones the press might call Bible-belt fundamentalists today. This group, the Pharisees, devoted their lives to following God. They gave away an exact tithe, obeyed every minute law in the Old Testament, and sent out missionaries to gain new converts. There was almost no sexual sin or violent crime among the Pharisees. They were model citizens.

Yet Jesus denounced the Pharisees.

Why? Of all people in Israel, weren't the Pharisees the type Jesus should have felt most comfortable with? His reaction shows how seriously he viewed a poisonous enemy that every young Christian runs into: legalism. The Pharisees had the idea that we earn God's acceptance by following a list of definable, external rules. To them, holiness could be measured.

Legalism is especially dangerous because on the outside it looks so respectable. It creates clean-cut, pure, pious followers of God. I first ran into legalism in an extremely conservative church when growing up in Atlanta, Georgia. It took only one month of attendance to figure out what the list of "don'ts" were in that church. The list included dancing, card-playing, smoking, drinking, civil rights, movies, rock music, long hair, games on Sunday, dice games, miniskirts, swimming with the other sex, and dating blacks or Hispanics. If you stayed away from all those evils and carried a Bible you were automatically accepted into the group.

Later in a Bible college in the South, I ran into a new list of rules. There, integration was supported (but still no inter-racial dating and, to stay on the safe side, the one resident black student roomed with the one resident Puerto Rican). Bowling, one of the Atlanta church youth group's favorite activities, was frowned on because some bowling alleys served liquor. Who would know whether you went there to bowl or to drink? Roller skating was forbidden, because skaters had the pernicious habit of holding hands while they skated and, besides, skating looked suspiciously like dancing.

The real hang-up at the Bible college seemed to be with sex. Miniskirts were not only frowned on, but measured! During the four years I was there, the acceptable skirt length rose from one inch below the knee to mid-knee to one inch above the knee (in the late sixties, when thigh-high skirts were everyday scenery elsewhere). Then the maxiskirt came along, and a great sigh of relief went up.

So innocent an act as a guy holding hands with a girl was banned. Handholders or especially kissers who were caught by a dean were quickly put on restriction or dismissed from school. One teacher went so far as to rail in class against lipstick, which to him was a sign of harlotry.

By talking with foreign students on campus, I discovered that overseas Christian groups have even more creative lists of sins. In South Africa, our Christian faith could be suspect if we chewed gum in public or prayed with our hands in our pockets. In some parts of France, a Christian who wears blue jeans is immediately distrusted.

Looking back, the Bible college rules seem sort of humorous, although they were enforced with an iron fist and rarely seemed humorous at the time. What is wrong with a denomination that bans dancing, buttons, or automobiles? It all sounds pretty innocent, hardly deserving of the strong words Jesus leveled at the Pharisees. Yet, the Pharisees were dangerous because they were so close to the truth. They believed in holiness, as God does, but they wanted the privilege of defining it. They snobbishly rejected any believers who did not follow their strict rules.

In some ways the legalists I met in Atlanta and Bible college were unlike the Pharisees. Few of them would have said that following their rules would earn God's acceptance. Yet they *acted* as if the rules were so important that God himself stood behind them. And they, too, tended to rate how "spiritual" people were.

Almost every Christian group has its own form of legalism. The dangers are so subtle that Jesus focused on them, spelling out the problems with legalism in Luke 11 and Matthew 23. They can be summarized this way:

1. *Legalism can be practiced for show.* When Pharisees prayed long hours, they made sure they were out on a street corner to be noticed. They wore unusual clothing to call attention to

how religious they were. The groups I was in never went so far as to require a specific uniform, as the Pharisees did, but I must admit the lipstickless, jewelryless, skirt-dragging Bible college girls were pretty easy to spot. The danger here, Jesus warned, is that those outer looks could cover up a lot of hidden problems that need dealing with. In my hall at Bible college were guys who had severe problems with guilt over masturbation, anger with parents and authorities, racial discrimination, hatred of some political groups. Somehow those things stayed undercover most of the time. We paid more attention to the visible things; we had to—a slip-up could get us expelled.

Jesus' first warning was against pride that legalism frequently produces. By obeying all the rules, Pharisees began believing they really were morally superior to other people. At Bible college I noticed how students would rate other schools: Wheaton College had just gone "liberal" by relaxing its rule against movies; Moody Bible Institute was tilting dangerously because it allowed such vices as holding hands as long as they were practiced off-campus. But we were still pure. We hadn't dropped our guard. We took a kind of perverse delight in how different we were.

2. *It breeds hypocrisy.* When rules are so clearly spelled out, it is easy to make the grade. Those who follow the rules soon relax in a sense of smug satisfaction, and it is easy to overlook hidden sins. Jesus said the Pharisees were like a cup that is clean on the outside and dirty on the inside. I could see the results of this in me and fellow students. We were too busy playing spiritual exercise games to show love and understanding to people who needed it.

I remember scores of sermons from my Atlanta church attacking civil rights and the Beatles. But I can't remember

I remember scores of sermons from my Atlanta church attacking civil rights and the Beatles. But I can't remember one against the bombing of a black church in Alabama.

UNHAPPY SECRETS OF THE CHRISTIAN LIFE

A PERFECT, EMPTY SHELL

one against the bombing of a black church in Alabama. And never from the pulpit did I hear a reference to the Holocaust in Germany, perhaps the most heinous crime in all history. This is what Jesus meant by his sarcastic remark, "They strain out a gnat and swallow a camel!" We were too busy measuring skirts to worry about war or racism or world hunger.

3. *It is addictive.* Legalism can be just as much a power game as climbing the corporate ladder, or climbing the social ladder in high school or college. In my high school, there was an unwritten game to see who could collect the longest list of school activities under his yearbook photo. The winner was rewarded with status and attention, a sense of power that he had beaten out all the rest. Jesus said that even spirituality can be misused like that.

Christians can flex their muscles at each other as a technique for pumping up their own egos, while they gradually grow callous toward others. The vice-president of a company who clawed his way to the top is likely to have little sympathy for the peons still beneath him: "I scrambled up the ladder; he can too." When someone in Bible college committed a blatant sin, the natural response was to judge and ostracize rather than to forgive.

4. *It lowers your view of God.* Legalists fool you. They are so dedicated, so obviously concerned with their faith that you would think they have a very high view of God. But the danger in legalism is that it lowers the sights. If my requirements as a Christian are spelled out in a rulebook, that is *all* I have to do. I can arrive. I can meet God's approval. The best legalists I knew felt secure and comfortable, like the Pharisees. They had fulfilled the law, had they not? But to those people Jesus shouts with a vengeance, "Fools!" No one ever *arrives* in the Christian life. We have to depend on God for the rest of our lives.

In summary, legalists miss the whole point of the Gospel,

If my requirements as a Christian are spelled out in a rulebook, that's all I have to do. I can arrive.

that it is a gift freely given by God to people who don't deserve it. Legalists try to prove how much they deserve God's love . . . . Assuredly, God is not impressed.

The rigid Old Testament law, Paul said, was like a schoolmaster to prove to us how far short of God we come. The law proves we cannot reach God, so God had to reach out to us, dying for us and restoring us to himself. Yet somehow legalists end up feeling more proud than grateful.

After studying Jesus' extensive treatment of the Pharisees in the two chapters I have mentioned, I tried to trace a common thread. I believe that all these characteristics are natural results of people who associate with each other all day. The Pharisees were simply around other Pharisees too much. They began competing with one another. By trying to impress each other with their love for God, they lost contact with the real enemy: Satan and his grip on non-Christians.

Is legalism quarantined to the Southeastern United States and isolated outbreaks in the world? No, legalism is like the common cold: no one is exempt. It quickly spreads through any group. I know Christians who think themselves more spiritual and enlightened than others because they feel free to drink wine and smoke pipes. But they have the same legalist problem.

A meticulous researcher named Merton Strommen surveyed seven thousand Protestant church youth from many denominations, asking them whether they agreed with the following statements:

"The way to be accepted by God is to try sincerely to live a good life." More than 60 percent agreed.

"God is satisfied if a person lives the best life he can." Almost 70 percent agreed.

" The main emphasis of the gospel is on God's rules for right living." More than half agreed!

It is as if the apostle Paul and Martin Luther had never opened their mouths! Christians still believe following a code of rules gets you to heaven.

This kind of thinking can prove fatal to a Christian's faith, and it may help explain a troubling phenomenon among

Christians. I have known dozens of kids who grew up in wonderful Christian homes and sound churches but decided later to junk their faith. After being outstanding examples of Christianity for a while, they became spiritual dropouts.

I have come to believe that many of them failed because they concentrated on the exterior, visible Christian life. When their Christian friends behaved a certain way and spoke a certain language, they began mimicking it. They became walking mirrors, reflecting all the correct styles and patterns of the church. Though there was no content to their faith, they were so skilled at following the rules that no one noticed the inside. Faith as an external exercise is very easy to cast aside, like a snake that sheds its skin. A person can discard a legalistic brand of Christianity just by trading it for a new set of rules, like those of Krishna Consciousness or Bahai or secular humanism.

If you develop Christian strength by focusing instead on the living Christ, it becomes much more difficult to shed.

Jesus did not, of course, teach that holiness is unimportant. But he carefully avoided legalism. Several times people asked Jesus for advice on a specific problem. Usually he wouldn't give a specific interpretation of an Old Testament rule; instead, he pointed to the principle behind a rule. He didn't tell a rich person to give away 18.5 percent of his goods; he said give them all away. He didn't define adultery as actual sexual intercourse; he pointed to the principle of using women as sexual objects so that men commit adultery in their hearts. Love? That is not an easy thing you can achieve among your friends. Jesus says, "I say, love your enemies!" Murder? "I have added to that rule," Jesus says. "If you are merely angry, even in your own home, you are in danger of judgment!"

I could develop a list of rules stricter than those of any Bible college. But Jesus specialized in wiping out legalistic obligations, saying, "No, there is much more than that." He never replaces my goals with something easier: he replaces them with something impossible.

It is not that Jesus doesn't care about how we live. He does care, and that is why he continues pointing out the lofty principles which should guide our lives. Jesus lashes out at legalism so that we will never pile up a list of credits on how good we are. The credit goes to God, not to us.

Christians use a word called "grace" that can be a cure for legalism. Grace simply means that God's love is freely given, with no strings attached. Grace is the exact opposite of legalism. Grace is what Jesus gave, and gives. Grace is the gift of Jesus himself.

It is hard for me to accept gifts. I am used to achieving because I work at something. I get good grades or make the tennis team or sell an article only if I drive myself. So it is difficult for me to accept grace, too. I would rather earn God's favor. But because of grace, I don't have to go around trying to impress God with how spiritual I am. Grace helps me to relax, to trust God, to realize he is already impressed enough to call me "a gift that he delights in" (Ephesians 1:11, *Living Bible*).

At a small group meeting in church I was profoundly reminded of the idea of grace by a strange, lonely guy named Josh McLynn. Josh would seldom look you straight in the face; he stared down, or sometimes over your shoulder in the distance. He always looked nervous, as if he were about to clear his throat. Josh said little, and I had tried to loosen him up by inviting him to the group.

The discussion that night was on what makes a Christian unique. One man mentioned how Christians are the only ones who have a reason for hope. The rest of the world, he said, have to spend life depressed since they couldn't be sure of an afterlife.

A woman talked about how Christians have so much happiness and peace. Another, a young girl, mentioned that Christians have higher standards than other people.

Josh McLynn sat silently through the discussion, occasionally scraping his feet in imaginary shapes on the floor. When I asked him about the evening, he didn't look up. He said, "Well, I always thought Christians were people who admitted they were sinners. The rest of us weren't supposed to have discovered that yet. But tonight, it seemed to me these folks were proud of their religion. It's like they think they're superior to me or something."

What Josh said cut me down. I had sat smugly through the meeting, proud of my articulate friends with all the answers. I began to see that I had again forgotten about the word *grace.* To a non-Christian, grace means that God's love is absolutely free: God accepts us just as we are. To the Christian, grace means that God is not finished with us yet—we are rough and unruly and cantankerous, but he still treats us as though we are the most beautiful of all his creations.

Somehow Christians tend to forget about grace. We become *proud* of our faith because it solves some of our problems and sets us apart from other people. We forget that, as Josh said, the only consistent difference between us and the rest of the world is that we have admitted we are sinners. The only good in us is a result of God's free grace.

Paul said, "Long ago, even before he made the world, God chose us to be his very own, through what Christ would do for us; he decided then to make us holy in his eyes, without a single fault—we who stand before him covered with his love" (Ephesians 1:4, *Living Bible*).

Sometimes it is hard to take God's free love. I keep wanting to impress him, to earn his respect on my own, like a muddied child bringing home a flower hoping mother won't notice the dirt. The amazing thing is, God doesn't notice the dirt. And that's hard to take. ▪

Two-Faced People

by Tim Stafford

■ I shall call him Mr. Thomas. He seldom missed church. He always prayed longer than anyone else and was most concerned about the "spiritual" dimensions of any problem. Yet he had cheated his relatives out of the family business, was a snoop, a liar, and to top it all off, overweight. Though I haven't seen him in years, I would still find it hard to enjoy shaking hands with him. He exuded slime. When I hear the word *hypocrite* I think of him.

Hypocrites are an easy excuse. Ask someone why he doesn't go to church, for instance, and you are likely to hear, "Because the church is full of hypocrites."

That answer helps him avoid saying, "Because I don't want to get up Sunday mornings" or "Because I don't believe in God the way Christians do" or even "Because I like my life the way it is and don't want to get close to something that might make me change." Any of these three, and plenty of others, would be decent reasons.

But someone who says the church is full of hypocrites puts his questioner on the defensive and doesn't have to deal with

Hypocrites:
For every group
they wear a different face.

the real issues. That is why I have heard this excuse so often. I have also heard many Christians stumble and hedge defensively when they hear it.

I overheard a non-Christian friend try a variation of it. When asked why he wasn't a Christian, he explained that he had been raised a Catholic. He described several things wrong with the nuns he had encountered: their uptightness, their severity, the mumbo-jumbo they pushed on him. He was hung-up with those nuns; that was why, he said, he wasn't a Christian.

The person asking the question then broke into a delightful laugh. "You mean," he asked incredulously, "that you're going to let a few little ladies in uniforms keep you from knowing God?"

Since I heard that, I have had an answer when someone tells me hypocrites keep him from becoming a Christian. I use the same incredulous response. "Are you trying to say that a few hypocrites are enough to keep you from meeting God personally?"

That helps deal with the excuse, leaving you free to talk about genuine issues. But aren't there times when hypocrites are a genuine issue? For most people they are just an excuse, but are they always? Even as a Christian I am bothered by the existence of hypocrites—people like Mr. Thomas. They raise troublesome questions. If Christianity is so wonderful, why aren't Christians more wonderful people?

Why is it you find liars in the same building where truth is exalted week after week? Why does the religion that praises honesty have phonies everywhere? It's as shocking as going into a presidential candidate's headquarters and finding that his workers plan to vote against him. The insincerity surrounding the candidate makes you doubt the candidate himself.

It is the real question, not the excuse, that I want to deal with here. Why are there hypocritical Christians, and what are we supposed to do with them?

A hypocrite might be called a counterfeit Christian, and that word sheds light. Why do people counterfeit something?

Only because that something is valuable. No one counterfeits a traffic ticket. No one fakes a bad report card. Only the more valuable things are counterfeited: things like twenty-dollar bills.

People will pretend to be rich. They will fake being university professors or football players. They will not usually pretend to be child beaters.

More than anything, people pretend to know God intimately. Why? Because knowing God is such a valuable thing, they want people to think they do. In a way, the presence of hypocrites demonstrates how desirable real Christianity is.

A generation ago, people would join the church because that was what all decent people did. Today, you don't lose respect if you don't go to church or claim to be a Christian. The only reason to be a hypocritical Christian is that you think knowing God is valuable.

I do not mean that hypocrites consciously calculate how to "counterfeit" Christianity. What is a hypocrite? He is someone trying to gain respect from every group he's in. Around Christians he acts spiritual, because that is what he thinks will make him admired. Around other circles he acts unspiritual, because that will win him admiration or power. He is a chameleon, colored by whatever environment he's in. Not having enough character to be himself, he is forced to try to live up to a set of contradictory standards.

Of course, he gains only misery. He doesn't fool many people for long. Christians are not the only ones disgusted by a hypocrite; even those who live unspiritually all the time look down on someone who tries to have it both ways.

So when I recognize a hypocrite, I have learned that the proper attitude is sadness. I am seeing a person who doesn't know who he really is. He is too weak to be consistent, and he is probably miserable.

It is one thing to know sadness is the proper attitude, and another to practice it. I think of Mr. Thomas again. I have a hard enough time loving family and friends. How am I to love this man, so repulsively false?

The only way is to see deeper into him: to see the misery in his soul, and also to see somehow the real person buried under piles of lies and fears. Somewhere inside must be the person God made.

But how can I ignore all the obvious faults in a Mr. Thomas? How can I discover the person God meant him to be if he can't discover it himself? I find that I understand someone like him only when I examine my own life carefully. When I look deeply into my own soul I discover that I am not much better than Mr. Thomas.

A hypocrite is someone who says he believes one thing but lives another. By that standard I am a hypocrite, and so are you. In fact, there is no one who claims to be a Christian who is not in one sense a hypocrite. Did not Jesus tell us, "You shall love the Lord your God with all your mind, soul and strength, and your neighbor as yourself?" And don't we agree that those words are the standard for life? But none of us lives up to those words. The greatest difference between me and Mr. Thomas is not whether or not I live up to my beliefs; on that score I am a failure too. The difference is in the attitude toward that failure.

Jesus once told a story about two men who prayed. The first man, a hypocritical religious leader, thanked God for the moral character he lived, which was considerably above the norm. The other man, a notorious crook, was so ashamed of himself he could barely speak to God. He did not thank God for anything. All he asked for was mercy. Jesus commented that the second man, not the first, was pleasing to God.

The man was not pleasing because he had sinned less, but because of his humble attitude. He knew his faults, and he didn't try to hide them.

I find that I only understand someone like Mr. Thomas
when I examine my own life very carefully,
looking deeply into my own soul.

Now, which of those two men do you think might have been cynical about a church where he could find hypocrites? The first man, obviously. He would not think of himself as a hypocrite—he lived a good life and was proud of it. He looked down on those who abused the Ten Commandments. He would consider himself too good to attend a church of hypocrites.

You can't imagine that attitude in the second man. He was so aware of his own faults that it never occurred to him to be offended by other people's. It is this attitude that pleases God, Jesus says.

When I hear that story, I try to place myself in it. When I am upset about hypocrites, am I not like the first man? But when I look deep into myself and see how far my own hypocrisy goes, I become more like the second man. Then, I don't have the courage (or the desire) to sneer at others—even at Mr. Thomas.

Each of us comes to Jesus as a starving man after bread. What does it say about me if I turn around to sneer at other starving men who don't yet know where the bread is?

Of course, one big obstacle to accepting hypocrites is that we find them in church. If I meet someone who is dishonest and mean in the grocery store I am not going to spit on him. But aren't Christians supposed to be different? Doesn't the Bible call Christians holy people? If so, why do churches tolerate hypocrites?

The answer is that most churches try not to. That is, they say loud and clear, almost every week, that dishonesty and selfishness keep us from really living. They encourage people

My only claim to "holiness" is that, time and time again,
I bring my hypocrisies and inconsistencies to Jesus.

to confront what is wrong with their lives. Some churches will take the extreme measure of expelling someone who consistently sins and won't admit it and change.

It is difficult to see what more a church could do. Is there a hypocrisy test we could give everyone? That begins to sound like the Inquisition. Frankly, I wouldn't want anybody else testing *my* hypocrisy. And I don't feel competent to judge anyone else's. Who really knows another person's heart? How can we tell what a person thinks when he's alone? We can evaluate what someone does, but how can we evaluate his sincerity? I would much rather leave that sort of judging to God. If I understand the Bible correctly, some of his judgments will turn out to be surprising to us.

Beyond that, I have to ask what a church is supposed to be. Are we to separate out the pure people and pack them into a building once a week? Or are we to have open doors to those whose lives are inconsistent and troubled?

The Bible calls Christians holy, but is that because they have resolved all hypocrisy and inconsistency in their lives? Not in my case. My only claim to "holiness" is that, time and time again, I bring my hypocrisies and inconsistencies to Jesus and allow him to forgive and renew me. That, I think, is all the holiness any of us will reach on earth.

I am thinking of Mr. Thomas again. He is a slimy character, but I don't know that God hasn't been working to change him. I don't know what he was like twenty years ago; it may be he had a long way to come. I can't compare his morality with someone else's; I can only compare it with what he would be like without God at all.

Nor do I know what Mr. Thomas is thinking inside. Maybe a severe crisis is right now bringing him back to the brink of change. I would not want to be the one who stepped in and condemned him the day before he gave in to God's urging.

But even if he never does change, what does it prove except that God wants us to be free? He wants an army of volunteers, not draftees. He will allow Mr. Thomas—or me— to go on in hypocrisy. He allows each of us the dignity to make up one's own mind. His only force is the subtle, steady pressure of his Spirit on our minds.

Since God allows freedom, there will always be hypocrites. He could force each of us, today, to come to terms with everything contradictory inside. If he did, I doubt many of us would have the strength to go on calling ourselves Christians. Instead, he brings our faults to us one at a time, and if we want to ignore them, we can. We can continue being hypocrites.

But when we do change our minds and let God's rule operate in our lives, he makes us free. We are free, most of all, to stop pretending that hypocrites are only *other* people. A hypocrite is someone hiding his problems inside, pretending they don't exist. A Christian is someone who has let his problems out and gives them, each day, to God. ∎